LETTERS TO THE BRAIN

JOHN B. KEANE

LETTERS
TO THE BRAIN

First published in 1993 by
Brandon Book Publishers Ltd
Dingle, Co. Kerry

British Library Cataloguing in Publication Data
Keane, John B.
   Letters to the Brain
   I. Title
   823.914 [F]

· ISBN 0 86322 157 2

Typeset by Brandon
Cover design: John Brady
Printed by: Guernsey Press, Channel Islands

Contents

Introduction 7

The Stomach Writes 13

The Posterior Writes 25

The Lips Write 33

The Knees Write 39

The Tongue Writes 47

The Hairs of the Head Write 55

The Memory Writes 63

The Fists Write 71

The Penis Writes 75

The Nose Writes 85

The Heart Writes 91

The Right Ear Writes 99

The Rear Aperture Writes 107

The Index Finger of the Right Hand Writes 113

The Eyes Write 121

The Guardian Angel Writes 131

The Sixth Sense Writes 141

The Conscience Writes 151

**Dedicated to Power's *Gold Label*
for sustaining me through the years.**

INTRODUCTION

Because I am the central point of the body it is fitting that I should be the one to write this introduction.

To some I may appear to be no more than a very ordinary depression in the middle of the abdomen but this is the whole point. The abdomen is the recognised centre of the anatomy and I am the centre of the abdomen. Therefore, I am the very core, the kernel, the centre of the centre. Let no one dispute my entitlement to authorship of the foreword.

In the matter of selecting the contributors for this long-overdue series of invocations I willingly leave myself open to criticism.

Let me say at once that this is purely a personal choice. I am certain that if the liver, the kidneys, the bladder or even the eyebrows, none of which are included here, were to nominate the contributors the selection would bear little resemblance to mine. This is to be expected; no two aspects or organs of the body are alike in either taste or temperament so that the last thing that should be expected of us is unanimity.

Nevertheless I have striven to be impartial and un-prejudiced in so far as it is possible for any appurte-nance of the human body to be. The reader will be familiar with other anthologies, treasuries and compendiums and will, no doubt, concur when I submit that any selection no matter how honestly or how painstakingly chosen is but a reflection of the anthologist's own personal philosophies, attitudes and convictions. This is not to proffer an apology for this selection; rather it is a justification.

Some of my fastidious readers will ask why the rear aperture? To this I say, why not? If this seems to be too simplistic an answer let me add that I personally find the area in question to be one of the less edifying regions of the body which I have the honour to represent as navel-in-residence, but I did not allow my personal squeamishness to militate against such a selection. I gave this particular choice a great deal of thought before I eventually decided in its favour.

The rear aperture, I told myself, is not my kettle of fish but the rear aperture, more than any other area of the body, has something to say and whether I like or dislike the tone, content or flavour of its pronouncements the rear aperture has a right to be heard, if only for the reason that what it has to say must perforce be vastly different from anything else we are likely to hear in the many splendid contributions which I have solicited over so long a period. I often, in fact, despaired of ever bringing my daunting task to a finish.

Others will ask, why not the breast nipples? They are

perfectly entitled to ask and I will endeavour to answer to the best of my ability. The breast nipples are near neighbours of mine and it must seem somewhat churlish to the gentle reader that I deliberately over-looked them when I was in the process of dispatching invitations to the selected organs and others.

Indeed the breast nipples are unobtrusive and yet sensitive. Together, in fact, we form an isosceles trian-gle and you cannot get much closer than that.

Other organs and aspects have offered themselves as contributors from the moment it became known that I had this undertaking in mind. Politely but firmly I de-clined every offer except those I had already chosen without reference to any authority save my own.

One of the great difficulties in compiling a work of this kind is having to reject a contribution which has been commissioned in good faith. Thanks to all the powers that be there was only one instance of this. I must confess that when I first invited the eyelashes to submit a contribution of roughly fifteen hundred words I had some misgivings. I had already accepted an important address from the hairs of the head and began to think that perhaps my readers might be put off by a surfeit of hairs. Add to this the fact that I was shamelessly importuned by the hairs which grow be-tween myself and the nether quarters to consider a rambling exposé which they maintain would truly titil-late the reader. Naturally I declined the offer. The contribution from the eyelashes exceeded in length all the other contributions put together although this was not the sole reason why the opus was returned to its author. In short it was downright boring and reeking with distasteful vanity. From its contents one would be forced to conclude that but for the input of the eyelashes there would be a total breakdown of the body's other components. I returned the bulky manuscript and suggested to its author that it should be published as a separate volume.

There are, I most willingly concede, many other worthy claimants for inclusion. There is the blood, the very stream of life, the saliva which plays a most important role and the lungs whose contribution cannot be measured. On the liquid side once more there is the urine, the perspiration, the tears etcetera, all worthy of inclusion but perhaps at this juncture I should emphatically stress that this is not a medical journal; rather it is a somewhat whimsical and often jaundiced series of onslaughts on the brain.

Another difficulty arose as I drew up the list of proposed contributors and this was, for me personally, the most serious dilemma of all. Should I, the navel, make a contribution or to put it another way was I, the navel, deserving of making a contribution. I might have consulted with others but in the last analysis I felt that the decision should be mine and mine alone. After a great deal of thought I decided against. In the first place my location has placed me next door to the epicentre of certain activities which would be more appropriate to the pages of a Sunday tabloid than the foreword of a book which may well appear in reputable bookshops and public libraries.

I live in the hope that some of the organs or aspects

which I have chosen for my selection will one day compile anthologies of their own and honour me beyond words by inviting me to contribute to theirs. I realise that I may have unwittingly omitted some who deserve to be included but I have diligently and ruthlessly scoured the anatomy and its invisible extensions lest I perpetrate an injustice against a deserving case.

Many may wonder why I could not find room for the backbone. The answer is that symbolically the backbone is fairly represented in the following pages. Another thing about bones is that they are associated with skeletons rather than living persons and Tom Scam, who is the personification of my brain, is a living person whose bones are still concealed by his all too mortal flesh. Finally, were I to include the backbone, there would be an avalanche of claims from other bones. In short, there are just too many bones.

Others will wonder why no muscle has been considered and this despite the fact that there are thirty score muscles in the body. My answer is, which muscle do you pick? Rather than offend the hard-working, industrious five hundred and ninety nine, I decided to choose no muscle at all.

The eyebrows I deliberately omitted because all eyebrows are cynics. It isn't that I dislike cynics but the eyebrows are the least articulate. All they can do is arch themselves.

Some may say that in writing this introduction I have deliberately masterminded a navel contribution. This is not so because I have not addressed myself to the brain as have the other contributors. What I have tried to do is to bring about a better understanding of the body's constituents and in addressing one brain I hope that the contributors will, as a consequence, succeed in addressing all brains and improve the general co-ordination without which the body must fail to function properly.

I think the book has succeeded in achieving what it set out to do in the first place, which was to alert the brain of one man to the fast-developing crisis in his body. I hereby extend my heartiest thanks to the contributors and wish them continuing success in their various undertakings.

The Navel.

THE STOMACH WRITES

Dear Brain,

I am your best friend. Never once have I broken faith. I came into the world a normal, healthy, hard-working maw and have survived until now without the slightest sign of ulcerous infiltration.

I have, for your pleasure and relief, calefacted ten thousand farts, no two of which have ever been exactly alike in volume or tone. I regard this as my greatest achievement. I have sent out into the world a selection varying from the sublime to the ridiculous, from the twittering to the grating, from the hushed to the explosive. Often strident and harsh they have shocked and stunned the sensitive listener. Other times they assumed pitches, lyrical and haunting, which no musical instrument could emulate.

These sounds are sometimes mistakenly taken for revelations or confessions of the posterus whereas, in point of fact, they are, as the street artist frequently proclaims, all my own work. It is I who creates. The posterus merely releases.

From my strife and turmoil come unmistakable expressions of joy and discontent, of anguish and elation. How wise was he who stated that there can be no great art without suffering and, certainly, you have made me suffer my share. Would that you had eaten like a normal man. I might have enjoyed a normal life but no! You always over-indulged. You could not and would not settle for your normal share. In the end I was obliged to come to the conclusion that true felicity is to be found only in starvation.

From that fateful moment when you first licked your young lips over being introduced to O'Shonnessy's sparkling cider I was to be flooded and overtaxed beyond my utmost capacity. There were times when, quite honestly, I thought I must surely burst.

Often you were forced into opening a second front. You were obliged to call the gullet into play during long periods of eructation.

How well I remember once after trying for hours to digest a massive intake of boiled turnips and gammon I gave up the unequal struggle and allowed nature to take its course. I recall it was at a residents' association meeting, a heated one if ever there was one, having to do with the manner of resistance which might be adopted to prevent the cutting of some dangerous and decaying trees in the vicinity.

Everybody had spoken but you. You sat stupidly in your chair unable to whisper much less to vociferate. Is anything more eagerly awaited, I ask you, than the utterance of a man who has kept his mouth shut whilst around him others are pontificating. There was silence as the chairman asked if you would like to make a contribution. It was the gammon and turnips, however, which did your speaking for you. They erupted into one of the loudest and most vulgar belches I was ever forced to initiate. The effect was the same as if there had been an unexpected clap of thunder. One anxious lady fled in terror from the chamber. The other females remained glued to their chairs fearfully awaiting a second eructation. The chairman, not fully aware of what had caused the explosion, made the sign of the cross and in a strangulated but solemn whisper entreated the immediate succour of the Three Divine Persons whilst others appealed to the Blessed Virgin not to desert them in their hour of tribulation.

When the initial shock had been absorbed you did the only decent thing possible under the circumstances. You rose, excused yourself and made your apologies to the chairman before exiting with a hand over your mouth lest a second explosion rock the building to its very foundations. You were never asked to speak thereafter.

Had you not come from healthy stock you would be feeding worms this long while. Fortunately for you, you were always possessed of a stomach which was capable, as your mother once boasted, of digesting an anvil.

On another occasion, after you had returned home with your wife from a dinner-dance, one of your neighbours claimed he was unexpectedly awakened from deep sleep. He had left the dance earlier like the sensible man of moderation that he was and was sleeping the sleep of the just when his slumber was disrupted. Granted the same fellow tends to exaggerate, but he positively swears that during dinner he saw you eating sufficient mashed potatoes and onions to keep a small army on the march for several days. According to the neighbour you left the kitchen where your wife was preparing some tea and took yourself to an outhouse. Here you were heard to belch so outrageously that the corrugated-iron roof of the outhouse was lifted several inches into the air in a veritable haboob of dust before settling once more on its supports. It was then that I was paid a belated but much-prized compliment:

"That man," said the neighbour, "has a stomach like a boa-constrictor."

Alas and alack I am at this time so grievously overworked that I would not be surprised if a duodenal ulcer was forming in the uproar of my digestion. It is truly a miracle that I have survived so long without succumbing to a cancerous tumour or to one of the other evil visitations to which all stomachs are subject.

If one of your more comprehensive belches could be fully analysed by a computer my story would be heard at last and you might come to your senses. If some sort of machine could be devised into which you might belch several times in the round of a day, and if a spoken interpretation could be forthcoming, I would a tale unfold that would bring tears from a hardboiled egg.

Please to remember during your more complacent

moments that I have been rumbling a long time now. Soon, all too soon, the lava will come spurting from your mouth and I shall be emptied forever. Yet, for all my rumbling and grumbling, my puling and my puking, my external navel area is the most presentable part of the entire anatomy. Even females who are averse to nude masculinity will reluctantly concede that the male belly is less obnoxious and more bearable than the buttocks, for instance, or the back or the chest or the callops, or indeed what have you! Let us, however, leave my outside to those who would have truck with it and let us return to the interior from which much is to be learned if one is prepared to listen. Listen to me my son and I will keep you healthy. The burp and the belch and all the revelations of the posterior, lisping or loud, must be given ear. These are my true sentiments and they contain much that will lengthen your days. I am the soul of patience. You have been stuffing me with impossible burdens of food and drink for the best part of a lifetime. By all the powers that be I should be out of commission long ago. I should have been supplemented, of course, by a second stomach or, at the very least, should have been rested for long periods. I never was, and this raises the question: how long more can I continue as I am? This is entirely up to you and, fortunately, it is not yet too late. Moderation will do both of us the world of good but moderation was never for you. You regarded moderation as a mortal enemy. You are a man who demolished two mature lobsters and a bottle of potstill whiskey for his forty-ninth birthday. In my youth I would have regarded such a monumental intake before bedtime as a mere repast, a challenge to my digestive juices, but nowadays I am put to the pin of my collar to cope with paté and toast.

I remember once aboard a train as you returned with a party of other drunkards from a rugby game the barman announced that all the bottled stout had been consumed. You resorted, as did your friends, to whiskey. Seated across the aisle was a mild-mannered book-immersed gorsoon whose mother dozed fitfully close by. As the whiskey mingled with a dozen or more bottles of stout and, of course, the prime fillet steak, the French fries, the onions and the mushrooms and the gases remaining from the morning's gin and tonics, there began a series of mild burps which gradually blossomed into boisterous belches.

I recall how I rumbled gently as the raw whiskey made you hold your breath before searing its way downwards into my crammed interior. There came from me, unsolicited by you, first a snarl followed by a whine, and then a succession of minor, almost inaudible rumbles. It was my way of intimating to you that enough was enough, that I needed to be rested. You persisted, however, and as though to keep me in my place threw back a glass of undiluted whiskey as if it were a spoonful of lukewarm soup. It was then that I held forth as I never held forth before. First came an inharmonious, low-key cacophony which increased in volume until all the passengers in the seats contiguous to yours lifted their heads in alarm, most notably the gorsoon who sat across the way. Not knowing where the sound came from his face registered considerable alarm. When I attained a crescendo of baying and howling the alarm was quickly replaced by fear and then abject terror. He leaped from his seat and sought refuge in his mother's arms. She, poor creature, disturbed from her unquiet dreams, bestowed upon him the absolute comfort of her arms as he called out to all within earshot that there were lions and tigers in the carriage.

You were obliged to beat a hasty retreat to the toilet where my rumblings eventually subsided. When you returned some time later your neighbours, drunken companions apart, had taken themselves well out of earshot and occupied some vacant seats at the far end of the carriage. It was not the first time you were responsible for an evacuation of this nature.

There was the occasion of the excursion and I think you will agree that this is the one incident of all the incidents in your life that you would most like to forget. At the time you were a mere eighteen and it was with considerable reluctance that you accompanied your mother who expressed a desire to spend a summer's day beside the sea. She prepared a lunch of chicken and salad which subsequently proved to be highly palatable as well as being extremely beneficial and easily digested. As soon as the lunch was consumed some elderly friends of your mother's happened along the beach. You excused yourself and informed her that you would like to have a swim and take in the amusements of the resort before returning to take her to the station. As a result it was not you but the contents of yours truly which were obliged to swim. These contents included the delectable salad so lovingly prepared by your mother, a large bag of periwinkles, a double portion of fish and chips before you started drinking and a second smaller portion when you felt peckish after you had drunk your fill.

At the time you were still a long way from graduation to beer and stout but you were a comparatively old hand as a dabbler in O'Shonnessy's sparkling cider, a beverage which you had been flooring successfully if excessively since your fifteenth birthday. Now in your eighteenth year you were to indulge to an unprecedented degree in what the manufacturers euphemistically labelled "the product of the home orchard, pressed out of mature and luscious fruit".

On the return journey you deposited your mother near the window in the front seat of the carriage directly behind the engine which was as far removed as possible from the carriage you had terrorised on the outgoing journey. You need not have bothered for the good reason that your victims had observed you as you entered the station and shrewdly waited for you to deposit yourself before availing of a carriage at the other end of the train.

Experience, like history, is a net from which it is difficult to extricate oneself but those homebound travellers should have learned from my rumblings and grumblings on the outward journey and should have extricated themselves at once from where they found themselves and awaited the arrival of the next transport.

All went well during the first few miles but then your brimming bladder began to expostulate and you relieved yourself in the toilet. It was here that you made the *faux pas* which was responsible for the disaster that followed. You had, in the tavern, out of sheer bravado, purchased a baby bottle of Jamaica rum which you concealed in your trousers' pocket to relieve, as you told yourself with a smirk, the rigours of the return journey.

How wise was he who said that you cannot put an old head on young shoulders. Unscrewing the cap you swallowed the entire contents of the baby rum. Such was the impact of this fresh intake that you found yourself panting for air.

But for a succession of breaths, long and deep, I would never have been able to retain that powerful Caribbean potion. Shaking your head and swallowing hard you drew yourself erect into a semblance of sobriety. The toilet, it transpired, was situated at the very end of that very last carriage and who should be seated in the seat outside but the same gorsoon you had routed on the rugby train. He made at once for his mother's lap, the naked fear rampant in his eyes. In the seats close by sat several other passengers, all alarmed, forewarned by the quaking boy and his anguished mother. Now, fully alerted to your presence, they sat rigidly upright in their seats.

For a moment you stood apologetically surveying them. You noted the pretty white frocks of the two genteel sisters in their early twenties and were hurt when they frowned upon seeing you. There was an elderly parson and his wife, a frail creature dressed in a leopardskin swagger of indeterminate age and a red bonnet weighted down by an assortment of multi-coloured wax fruits. Finally there was a trio of nuns, hooded and veiled with beads in their hands as they silently recited the evening prayers.

As you stood uncertainly, unable to make up your mind whether you would be capable or not of maintaining your balance, you were suddenly suffocated by a feeling of nausea. Then came the upheaval prompted by the earlier and injudicious intake of the Jamaican rum. A torrent of cider issued in wanton abandon from your open mouth. In it was the undigested flotsam of periwinkles, chips, fish, chicken, salad and every other particle in my beleaguered depths. It would be the vastest and most drenching vomit you would ever make and I say this knowing you to be a veteran of a thousand upheavals. What an ecumenical puke it was! It equally drenched the Roman Catholic nuns and the Church of Ireland parson as well as his horrified wife. The end of the stream which contained the majority of the undigested French fries and all of the barely chewed fish was distributed evenly over the mother and son and the pretty white dresses of the mortified sisters.

Still spewing the remains of the record-breaking retch you lurched forward without as much as a word of apology leaving in your wake a vomit-covered and utterly shattered company of innocents who between them, the clergyman apart, had never consumed as much as a solitary pale sherry in their entire lives.

They sat now reeking in unfamiliar filth, too stunned to utter the slightest protest. The clergyman was the only person to pass comment. Imagine my surprise to hear a man of the cloth suggest that it was I, the stomach, which was to blame for the entire catastrophe. Said he in a voice shaking with destain:

"The scoundrel can't stomach his liquor!"

To associate me with the appalling misbehaviour of my proprietor was an injustice of the greatest magnitude and to think that it came from the mouth of a uniformed Christian. It was you, the Brain, who was totally responsible and it was you, you craven coward, who slyly departed the scene when the damage was done.

The fact that I have survived intact to this day is ample testimony to my mettle. I am, however, prepared to forget the past. There is little profit in remembering ancient wrongs although I can never quite erase the sight of those genteel people endeavouring to clean themselves as you sneaked drunkenly to the leading carriage.

The tragedy was compounded by the fact that they had believed themselves to be safe. I believe that Robbie Burns created the most truthful and profound stanza of all time when he leaned on his plough to address himself to the mouse whose habitation he had unwittingly destroyed:

"The best laid schemes of mice and men
Gang aft agley
And leave us nought but grief and pain
For promised joy."

23

How blissfully they sat before you were called to the toilet, and then in a thrice how shattered! I could recall for you other indiscretions but the excursion puke as I would like to call it is sufficient for our purpose. It is now high time you came to your senses.

Look then to my upkeep and maintenance and spare me henceforth from the indigestible and the unpalatable. I will reward you well for it is true to say that when I fail you everything else will fail you as a matter of course. Remember this when next you tax me. I cannot go on forever; time to wind me down; to give me the rest I so richly deserve or I will growl you out of your appetite and groan you into an early grave.

Sincerely,

Your Stomach.

THE POSTERIOR WRITES

Dear Brain,

What a shapely and ornamental article I was in my heyday! How rotund and fulsome, how firm yet buoyant, how curvaceous yet slender! Oh how eminently patteable was I, how kneadable, how carressable! how trim! I was as shapely a backside as ever adorned the end of a trunk, as ever overlooked a thigh or collop, as ever saucily sported itself before the eye of misfortune!

How I scorn the term buttocks; they remind me of so much dead meat.

They have labelled me bum, bottom, backside, arse, croup, rump and coccyx but what care I! I am what I am, a simple posterior designed to enforce the rut, to break the fall, to suffer the kick, to steady the scrum, to sit on the fence, to press the case, to soften the shock, to bear the brunt.

I have been threatened with more kicks and, perversely, invited more kisses than any other part of the anatomy. Alas, I have received too many of the former and none of the latter. I doubt if it will ever be resolved whether posteriors were just made to be kicked or whether the brain draws the kicks upon us. It's like trying to decide which was there first, the hen or the egg, the whore or the pimp. I have watched silently as our own feet, left and right, aimed themselves after a retreating posterior whose owner had been agressive or insulting. Similarly I have seen you kick a bending figure on the rear end for no reason at all. I heard you justify your actions afterwards by suggesting that as surely as stones were made to be flung so were arses made to be kicked; your very own words my dear lord and master.

Unlike Gaul I am only divided into two parts. Yet there exists no partition for we are really one. Can you imagine a posterior with only one cheek? Could anything be more ridiculous? I remember the first kick which ever jolted me into the harsh realities of co-existence. You were but a ten-year-old whilst the man who kicked me was eighty. Much as I resented that kick it was, I felt, richly deserved. You had callously taken the life of one of this three ducks, the remnants of a once populous clutch which he had vainly hoped would provide him with eggs for his daily needs. The stone which you flung would not normally arrive within an ass's roar of the target but on this tragic occasion the duck was smitten on the very top of its head. Death was instantaneous. You were caught in the act and the old man implanted a kick which you were to feel for several weeks afterwards. That was the first of many.

Kicks, however, I could accept but not permanent disfiguration which was to be my lot when you reneged on your fees in a seedy massage parlour. Before you had time to draw on your trousers the madame, quick as a flash, inscribed the sign of the cross with a razor blade on my left cheek where the mark remains to this day as a caution to masseuses everywhere that they were not to be duped by your innocent face but were to demand their fees in advance.

Some months later as your mother handed you a towel in the bathroom she could not help but notice the transverse lacerations which dominated my left cheek. Shocked beyond words she demanded an explanation. Hastily wrapping the towel around me, thereby concealing the crude disfiguration, you explained without batting an eyelid that it was part of an initiation ceremony. Inveterate liar that you were you convinced the poor woman that you were now, as a result of the sacred inscription, a member fully-fledged of a society devoted to the propagation of the Catholic faith, a society which expressly forbade its members to wear their hearts on their sleeves but rather wished them to pursue their vocations secretly and discreetly. You brought tears to the poor woman's eyes when you explained that the reward for such unselfish devotion would come not in this life but in the next. She never doubted you and you salved your conscience by convincing yourself that you wished to spare her the seamier side of your more mundane activities.

As the years rolled by and your paunch began to

protrude so did I begin to obtrude in the opposite direction until the specially tailored slacks and trousers which fitted your once lithe figure so admirably had to be disposed of for good to be substituted by the baggy britches which are anathema to females. Drink was the chief reason for my expansion. You might have held the obesity at bay had you moderated your intake and indulged in jogging or even walking, although my innate honesty compels me to recount an isolated occasion when you ran several hundred yards without stopping until your goal was attained.

You had dined well, as I remember, but then there was never an occasion when you did not dine well. On the evening in question, while the stomach laboured incessantly to digest the beef, the pudding, the potatoes, the assorted vegetables, the gravy, the sweet and the cheese, you fell into a deep slumber in front of the sitting-room fire. Around you sat your loving family, your well-preserved, pseudo-aristrocratic wife and charming daughters. Your gentle snoring soon dominated all the other sounds of the room. After a while the snores grew fitful and uneven. Your wife, believing you to be the victim of a nightmare, called into your ear that there was no need for alarm. When you spluttered into wakefulness she repeated the assurance.

"No need for alarm!" you echoed in consternation as you noted the hands of the mantelpiece clock. The time was twenty minutes to eleven which was the precise and blessed hour the taverns closed their doors for the night. You leaped from the armchair like a scalded cat and without donning hat or overcoat dashed out of doors and ran through the streets like a man demented until you reached the nearest pub.

If I were ever asked to nominate that part of your body which was subjected to the most exercise I would, without hesitation, declare wholeheartedly for your right elbow although that same elbow has added, you might say, to my dimensions more than anything. I recall a particular night when the circumference was extended by a full inch, most of which accrued to me. You drank several pints of beer, retired to a hotel where you ordered a mixed grill which contained all the orthodox constituents from chop to liver, but which in this instance was enriched by several medallions of black and white pudding. You salivated and snorted like a starving hyena. The proprietor of the hotel was so taken by your appreciation that he added several further medallions of the puddings in question. Alas, because of their saline contents you consumed another half gallon of beer.

I just cannot forgive you for repeatedly indulging yourself in such a gluttonous fashion. You have made me ungainly and obese. Bad as this is the worst of all is that nobody cherishes me. You have never uttered a single word in praise of me or a word in my defence. There are no poems or songs about me or my equals. The only praise I ever received was when I accidentally came in the way of a kick at goal during a football game. Somebody shouted from the sideline, "Good arse!" Beyond that nobody ever singled me out for approbation. I have no dignity. It's been eroded over the years by your failure to keep me in shape. I once had innate dignity and when innate dignity is eroded there is no substitute. Acquired dignity is less sensitive.

I am often mildly irked by the veneration which is accorded to my female counterpart – it seems to be an object of immeasureable esteem as well as being a powerful source of titillation and infatuation. Men are frequently quite carried away by moderately attractive female posteriors and just as you slobber over your food so do the lecher and the philanderer slobber over the curvaceous sit-me-down of the graceful female. In fact I recall an occasion after you had emerged one morning from a newsagent's in the metropolis, you were so attracted by the pair of bouncing female buttocks in front of you that you followed their proprietress blindly for over a mile until she disappeared through a doorway. Granted the female posterior is smooth as silk, eminently hand-cuppable and more capable of exciting the male on-looker than any other aspect of the female make-up. There is simply nothing to compete with it. Woe is poor me by comparison. Many a worshipful devotee will tell you that of all the world's vistas the female fundament is the most surpassing whereas even the most chaste will not deny that, in all its unclad glory, it is the most intoxicating of prospects. But enough! I digress too much.

I have, for too long, succumbed to base matters. How can one be analogical when one descends to the very bottom! Despite my lowly position, however, I must not despair. I cannot draw myself up nor can I alter my situation. Yet I am strangely content. I do what is required of me and I believe I do it well. Little is seen of me and maybe that is just as well. All exposure has ever done for me has been to bring ridicule down upon me. I can still hear the derisive whoops from the day the seam of your trousers burst when you stopped to tie your shoelace as you searched for a Christmas turkey in the market place. You slunk home with your inadequate hands vainly trying to cover the exposed area which was the title bestowed upon me by your kind-hearted mother. I am, I must painfully conclude, an object of derision. I do not deserve to be, hairy though my lineament may be and coarse my features, with a central situation which does little to enhance my over-all appearance. If I were permitted to choose my epitaph it would read as follows:

"Faithful down below he performed his duty.

No posterior deserved more to be raised aloft."

If I could leave my impression, my mark as it were, upon this paper I would be proud to do so, so that maybe one day a discerning soul might read my lines as the clairvoyant reads the palm and tell the world of the vilification to which I have been subjected and declare the true warmth, the true loveliness that I exude. If posteriors have a dream then mine would be to hold myself up to a mirror and ask:

"Mirror, mirror on the wall,

Who is the fairest of us all?"

To which the mirror would instantly reply:

"Thou art, oh arse!"

Remember, dear brain, that dreams sometimes come true. All you have to do is address yourself to moderation and unremitting exercise and I might be transformed into a posterior, trim and shapely, which might be exhibited in public as a shining example of my kind.

Sincerely,

Your Posterior.

THE LIPS WRITE

Dear Brain,

There was a milkman, a curly-haired, chubby-faced fellow who might, to the casual onlooker, have seemed twenty when he must really have been sixty at least. He was that kind of person. Age, it would seem, made little impression upon him. Your father had known him for years, or so he used to say, which means the man might have been eighty. His fountain of youth was his whistling. First thing in the morning, after the cocks had crowed and the last of the rooks had flown, his exhilarating serenading could be heard as he cycled upon his round.

What a happy man he must have been! He never whistled a drab melody. He excelled at the stirring march and he would empty his heart to nurture the sweet chords of love which he warbled, free of charge, morning after morning for all and sundry.

Dour veterans of the marital confrontation relented and turned in their beds to celebrate sweet sessions of amorous rapture and all because of this incidental input. The morning was transformed into a backdrop for his princely rendition. He contributed more to the rescue of foundering marriages than any human inter- mediary could ever hope to, and not unwittingly I might add.

It often seemed to us lips that he was transported here from some heavenly sphere for no other purpose than the upraising of downcast hearts. How I secretly yearned that you, one day, would purse us into an in- strument which would fritter away depressions and upraise the human spirit to its loftiest pinnacles!

Surely the pipings of that dear departed milkman had their roots in his immortal soul, and yet it was the orifice of the contracting lips that modulated and measured the bewitching torrent of empyreal sonority which charmed and delighted all those fortunate enough to be within earshot. We, too, might have at- tained to such fluency had you but persevered after your early failures. There wasn't a child in the street who did not try to emulate that milk-carrying maestro.

We remember once of an icy morning how he fell from his rickety bicycle, spilling the contents of both his pails and breaking two front teeth into the bargain. Poor fellow, his lips were brutally lacerated. The tears formed in his eyes as the white streams of freshly- drawn milk coursed irredeemably towards the nearest channel, but how quickly he transformed misfortune into triumph.

Supporting himself on his right knee and placing his left hand over his breast he pursed his shattered lips, oblivious to the agonising pain. Then, extending his right hand to his invisible public, he gave the performance of his life. That rendition of "At the Balalaika" was the performance for which he would always be remembered. Not even the combined efforts of Nelson Eddy and Ilona Massey in their illustrious heydays succeeded in wringing such total ecstasy from this immortal lovesong. Long before he finished, the underemployed lips of that once dreary street were never so utilised in pursuit of loving fulfilment, and to think that it was a simple pair of mutilated lips which created the mouthpiece through which this masterpiece was delivered. For the listening lovers in the silent houses it was a never-to-be-forgotten experience. Some had never even dreamed of aspiring to such unprecedented ecstasies. Remember their moment came only after years of waiting. If the world and its people could only wait long enough everybody would, eventually, be kissed by someone, be loved by someone.

However, we lips were not designed for whistling alone. On a more realistic level we accurately direct the airflow that cools the steaming soup, the scalding tea, the gum-blistering stew. Alternatively, we warm the freezing fingers with the comforting breath, but it is at kissing that we excel.

Kissing can be a precarious business, as many a rueful participant will verify. We were designed to kiss and we are capable of producing a true multiformity of kisses. Our kisses may be blown and wafted from our pouting embouchure by the eyes or by the hands, but the imposition of lip upon lip conceals more hazards than thin ice on a bottomless lake.

Lips love to kiss but we also kiss to love and this must never be forgotten by those who would recklessly disburse kisses at every hand's turn. "A kiss on the brow for the dead we loved," your late and pious father used to say. "A kiss on the cheek for a friend but a kiss on the lips," quoth he, "is the most imponderable of all propositions and should never be undertaken lightly, especially by those who foolishly presume they are fully aware of the dangers involved."

In its own time and in its own place and in conditions blessed by love the kiss will melt the icicles of frigidity and replace the pinched cheek with the amorous suffusion. Of all the earth's moistures there is none so delicate as that of the lips nor can the subtlest velvet match their smoothness of texture. When poised to kiss there are no dewier petals on land or sea.

We, your very own lips, are ambassadors from the court of true love and deserve the respect and deference which are the dues of all accredited envoys. Sully us not by debasement or defilement and do not ever shape us for the spit of ridicule, foulest of all human ejaculations; neither pout us for the contemptuous grin, but be aloof and restrained so that we may buttress your dignity and beautify your wrinkling face.

Be not an imitator of posterior windbreaking but whistle cheerfully in the dark for the benefit of those who may be affrighted. We have served you well and will continue to serve but we are a sensitive pair and would remain pursed rather than be party to grins and grimaces which may hurt another.

You have, alas, imposed us on the lips of females we would rather have shunned and disgraced us by not imposing the gentlest and sweetest of kisses upon the fair face and virgin lips of the lovely Lily Lieloly. Still and for all we are prepared to light for you the golden lamp of love, preserving its mellow glow through all your days and nights and trimming it to last your fretful pace till the final Amen is murmured!

In your lifetime, dear brain, you have kissed far and wide. Be thankful for your share and pity the lips starved of kisses. How goes it in the ancient ballad:

'Tis I my love sits on your grave,
And will not let you sleep
For I crave one kiss of your cold, cold lips
And that is all I seek.

Yes indeed; that is all he sought, poor fellow, and you who are blessed with a living wife and who knows not the pain of loss may kiss when you choose and yet would kiss elsewhere and put your lips for auction to the first bidder. You remind me of the improvident mule who vacates a barely nibbled pasture for the promise of sweeter clover behind the next hill, but then, in matters hymeneal, you could never see the wood for the trees. Would you had piped sweetly but once in your lifetime, rather than the chirpings cheap and lewd wasted upon the passing lass. Unmusical and unromantic crow, you never turned a solitary female head whereas the true whistler serenading from his soul wooed the delicate ear and won the most precious heart. We, your lips, are God-given and whether we pout, whistle or kiss, we remain yours to do with as you will, but we would beseech you to employ us in order to issue the sweet whisper rather than formulate the braggart shout which shatters the female ear and dispatches discord like a raging fever through your house and every house.

The sweet whisper is the very distillation of love's gentle presence and we would have you know that we have responsibility for the processing and distribution of all whispers, sweet and secret, long and short; therefore, engage us unreservedly in this respect and you will be as well rewarded as we will be fulfilled. Where shouting, threats and posturings fail, a whisper carefully wrought and intimately delivered by the lips will always succeed. When our modifying sensitivity is bypassed by the shout and the scream respect is shattered and civility dies.

Look to your lips, dear brain, and the harmony that is absent from your life shall be implanted. We shall infuse in you the fire that shines through the spirit of love and when we part there shall be revealed for the first time the smiles of which you were always capable but never uncovered to a world in dire need of a produce so refined. We should, perhaps, now draw to a close. We look forward to better times and to remaining firmly closed in the face of unjust criticism and broadsides of a malicious nature.

Sincerely,

Your Lips.

THE KNEES WRITE

Dear Brain,

Our fondest memory is supporting the lovely Lily
Lieloly when she sat on your lap in the rear seat of a
motor car as you journeyed home from a dance one
blissful summer's night many years ago. We were
proud to give service to one so splendid and innocent.
Although the journey took over an hour we never
flinched and, if needs be, would have happily borne
her till the pleasurable commission made us numb.

Later you were to use us for the transportation of
creatures infinitely less savoury and immeasurably
more seductive but our fealty was and ever will be to
Lily Lieloly. Had we but wings to fly we would one day
bear her safely to the very portals of heaven. For her
part, unlike so many others, she never made us feel
knobbly or unsolicited. We regarded ourselves, in fact,
to have been devised for the sole purpose of minister-
ing to her in matters of transport. Enough of Lily,
however.

We recall with dismay the countles times we wobbled as you trundled homewards in your cups. We became scarred and battered beyond recognition when you would stagger, then stumble and finally fall, sometimes on your posterior, other times on your hands but more often than not on us poor knees.

We knees are ungainly enough without adding to our aesthetic inelegance. Whatever it is about knees and despite their undeniable usefulness to men and women, nobody seems to love them. We have never heard it said of a man that he has lovely knees and rarely indeed would you hear it said of a woman. Women in fact, from what we manage to gather whilst listening to their conversations, very often loathe their own knees, particularly if they are unusually knobbly, crinkly or over-convoluted. It does not matter that we play the role we were ordained to play and that without us there would be no footloose movements of any consequence. Out of commission we spell total stagnation and, even when we suffer minimal damage, travel by Shanks mare is restricted.

Once we felt you fall clumsily on us when you were swearing love to a rather podgy-faced woman at a distant orgy. You very nearly permanently damaged us, so heavy was this infatuated collapse, this prurience-inducing gratulation, this dastardly declaration of lunatic libidinosity. More offensive still was the raucous and unladylike laughter of your pickled pick-up as she contorted herself drunkenly in appreciation of your loutish tomfoolery. We were sore for several days following that particular exhibition.

We recall with delight how you were overcome on the occasion by your own alcoholic fumes and were unable to perform.

We would now like to refer you to a function for which we were, we firmly believe, designed by God. This is for the sublime purpose of paying Him the homage that is His eternal due, although you would argue in drink that if you were invited into the world and given the choice of acceptance or refusal you would have declined the invitation and stayed where you were, wherever that was.

You were always a great man for flying in the face of God, forgetting, you poor benighted mortal, that you may one day have to crawl on your hands and us in supplication before His throne, and that day may not be as far away as you think. Now to that function for which we were specially designed; i.e., making you to kneel in prayer. Alas it is the one function for which we were never even partially utilised and it is the one function in which we would have been pleased to involve ourselves. It was Saint Paul who said: "At the name of Jesus every knee should bend."

Paul was, of course, referring to the followers of Christ and must surely have meant every Christian knee, two of which have been possessed by you since the day you were born. However, neither of us can recall anything remotely approaching the faintest semblance of a genuflection since your sinless and virtuous mother was borne away to the plains of heaven by the nine choirs of angels. Neither did you kneel to pray at the anniversaries of your parents' deaths.

Although these were not deliberate sins of omission we, nevertheless, find your negligence to be bordering on the unforgiveable.

How is it that your late father could always manage to find time for prayer, always make it a point to bend us on the floor or the pavement or in the fields which he loved to traverse in obeisance to his heavenly benefactor! How often we foolishly wished we were his knees instead of yours but those were transient aspirations for, through thick and thin, we are still determined to support you and though somewhat rickety and wobbly we will persevere with the struggle to support your ever-extending paunch and inexorably fattening buttocks and thighs.

We lovingly recall your father as he would gently lower himself into a kneeling position to thank the appropriate saint for some favour received. Even when he would recover the pipe or the spectacles which had been mislaid for but a few moments he would cross himself and kneel in thanksgiving.

The only occasion in recent times that we remember you kneeling in real earnest was when the right knee of one of your enemies guilefully connected with that prized and sensitive area commonly referred to as your private parts!

At once you fell to your knees clutching the affected spot, uttering hideous screams and gasping for breath until you were stretchered away to the nearest infirmary by some of your cronies. Even they would not deny that you had at last come into your entitlement for you, in your day, were never slow to inflict the same punishment on those who had incurred your wrath! How true the old adage: "Those who live by the sword shall die by the sword."

You didn't die then but you knelt as you never knelt before and, alas, have not knelt since nor have you the slightest notion of kneeling. We beg you to do so before a day dawns when infirmity will preclude any possibility of your kneeling and that will be the time you will want to kneel most so that your supplications for salvation will be properly delivered. Tennyson, to whom your father was devoted particularly towards the end of his days, asks:

For what are men better than sheep or goats
That nourish a blind life within the brain,
If, knowing God, they lift not hands of prayer
Both for themselves and those who call them
    friend?
For so the whole round earth is every way
Bound by gold chains about the feet of God.

You would do well to utilise us more while we are willing and able to accommodate any prayerful postures you may hopefully adopt before it is too late.

We have been most wrongfully deprived of our right to participate in divine worship. Millions and millions of knees fullfil their proper roles every Sabbath while we languish and pine for our heritage.

I don't know for sure how medical texts might describe us but more than likely we would be delineated as being joints of the ginglymus type in the middle part of the human leg. We are the articulation between the femur, tibia and the patella. This is what they have to say about us in medical journals but this is a somewhat clinical analysis. There is much more to us that has not been revealed by the followers of Hippocrates.

In all wars from the lowly skirmish to the decisive battle the knees have played vital roles. Without us every rifleman who ever aimed his weapon would be at a disadvantage. Remember the position favoured in extended-order infantry drill in which the soldier kneels on the right knee, rests the left forearm across the left thigh and grasps his rifle in the position of order arms with the right hand above the lower hand. It is we who are at the very nub of this manoeuvre. Upon our mobility depends the very life of every soldier in charge or retreat.

It is we who enable the thirsty traveller to kneel by the roadside spring and it is we who stiffen to attention when the anthem of our country is sounding and yet we cannot recall a poem or song in praise of knees, but then it is also true that the horse which earns the oats rarely receives them. We care not because we know that virtue is its own reward and we are content while we are able to serve.

We had hoped – oh! impossible dream – that one day you would be summoned into a royal presence and honoured for services to your fellow man. We saw ourselves bending so that you might kneel upon the tasselled mat. For us this truly would have been a moment to cherish. Only a knee can kneel and kneeling is the *sine qua non* of knighthood. Then would come the laying on of the royal sword followed by the royal command, Arise Sir Knight!

Sir Thomas Scam. It sounds right and proper but alas your activities over a lifetime were more suited to the jailyard than the palace. In fact there are many who would suggest that you should be permanently incarcerated, roundly whipped every day and made to lie on beds of nails at night. We must be thankful that nobody ever suggested you should be made to kneel upon broken glass.

We now feel obliged to conclude, and still we entertain the hope that you will see fit to make more use of us at wayside shrines and ancient oratories, before the sacred tabernacle and representations of the crucifixion, in cemeteries and places of holy pilgrimage, in mosques, synagogues, pagodas and temples of every denomination, in grand cathedral and humble chantry. Avail of us we beseech you so that you might give thanks to your creator for the life He has breathed upon you and for the longevity He has thus far granted you. Weigh upon us in every holy place and make it known to the giver of life that for every breath you are grateful to Him and mindful of His unparallelled munificence, for life is the father and the mother of all gifts and cannot be estimated in human terms. Press upon us then without delay so that we may contribute to your belated atonement and ultimately share in your salvation.

Sincerely,

Yours Knees.

THE TONGUE WRITES

Dear Brain,

It was I who was obliged to deliver the utterance which contained the first lie you ever told. It was a deliberate falsehood devised to ingratiate yourself into your mother's good books after she had chastised you following a fit of petulance.

You had been sent to your room like many a small boy before you. It was a job I detested and as you know by now I can be a very sensitive fellow indeed with the power to react when an injustice is perpetrated against me. As you lay in your room endeavouring to count the myriad patterns of wild oats on the wallpaper you hit upon a plan which very nearly proved to be the death of your mother. You staggered from the bedroom clutching your breast, announcing in tones of agony from the top of the stairs that you were going to die. You blundered unsteadily downwards towards the hallway to where your mother had hastened from the garden where she had been engaged in the pruning of rose bushes. She was at first petrified upon hearing your screams and then spurred into action like all mothers by concern for your safety.

Upon beholding you she instantly fainted but luckily for all concerned her collapse coincided with the visit of an itinerant chimney-sweep who ministered successfully to both of you, to your mother by gently slapping her face and to you by stoutly implanting the toe of his wellington fairly and squarely upon your pampered posterior.

How often has it been said that a kick in the right place often put a man on the right road! Certainly it was true of that occasion for you never employed such a dangerous form of deceit on your poor mother again.

You were, however, to dupe her and others in a complexity of ways for the remainder of your life. How frequently have we heard it said of scandal-mongers that their tongues should be cut out. I am just another organ and, therefore, for everything I say you must be held responsible. You dictate to me and I articulate. I fulfil my other roles as a matter of course. I concern myself with assisting the teeth and throat in the vital acts of chewing and swallowing. My mucous membrane attaches itself to food, sloshing it through gum-induced saliva, retaining and refining it for the tittivation of my tastebuds and at the end of these pleasurable proceedings dispatching it gratefully past the tonsils, my roots and down the deep throat to the receptive stomach.

I am filled with the most sensitive nerve fibres which

issue rebukes and warnings to the entire nervous system as well as the mouth. From my fold to my papillae to my apex I am involved in essential activities for the betterment of the body as a whole and while I do not wish to sound boastful I believe it could be argued that I am an organ who bears great responsibilities as a contributor to the well-being of any given human.

I could go on about my physical philanthropy but these functions I have cited are as nothing in comparison to the awesome power which sends millions of words tripping off my apex day after day. Most of these I will concede are meaningless and although packaged in phrases and sentences it can be safely said that were they never uttered there would be no loss whatsoever to the world. There are countless men and women who have utilised me on a round-the-clock basis and who have never issued a word of common sense. There are millions who use me for nothing better than criticising and maligning friends, neighbours and institutions. There are, mercifully, a gracious and godly few who never employ me for the voicing of evil commentary about others and but for these kind-hearted souls the world would be a more damnable place than it already is. Their example stands out like sweet birdsong in a shadowy grove. As for those who employ me for the distribution of the truth they slash through hypocrisy and cant the way a comet sears through the heavens at night, and yet they do not wound or maim nor do they use the truth for their own advancement. Indeed they wound themselves more by adhering to it, cut themselves adrift from the safe anchorage of convention and expose themselves without raft or lifebelt to the hostile seas of suspicion.

I remember a female teacher, one of the few who refused to be taken in by your pretended illnesses. When you blamed another boy for your own piddle-stains on the freshly whitewashed gable of the school-house she requested you to stick out your tongue so that the world might see the black mark on its surface, proof if any was needed that you were already at that tender age an unrepentant liar.

You obdurately refused to exhibit me in public. Now I am an organ which never entertains aspirations towards vanity and thrusting me forth in public, medical examination excepted, is not my idea of fun because I am not in the least pretty or personable. The better organs never are.

However, on that occasion I fervently wished that you would for we tongues have properties with which we suffuse ourselves and were you to make a spectacle of me on that occasion I would have been as black as the bottom sod in a raised peat bank.

Organs are not capable of acting independently of the brain but they are capable of reacting, often with embarrassing consequences.

There are many men who believe that it is both proper and natural to tell lies to women and indeed they believe that those who tell the truth to wives, especially, are leaving the side down, as it were. Fortunately most women do not believe daylight from the opposite sex who would use them for their own ends. I once heard your own wife admonishing your daughter for believing what she had been told by a neighbourhood rapscallion. Said your long-suffering spouse on that memorable occasion:

"My dear, you are not to believe a word of it and from now until the day you die you are not to believe a single word you are told by a man, especially a married man."

Would that more females had adopted your wife's sensible philosophy. It is impossible to estimate the amount of anguish they would have been spared and more difficult still to measure the volume of tears that would be left unshed. Of the two known sexes man is the bigger liar. Ask any tongue for confirmation and I will be borne out. In fact the more daring of the males will invent the most outrageous lies to save themselves, to justify an injustice, to convince themselves that wrong is right and to seduce and subsequently ravish innocent females.

I know what I'm talking about. All too often have I uttered your distortions against my will. Right down through history man has shown himself to be the master of the big lie. It succeeds, though not for all time, when all else fails. It is easy enough to convince a gullible public; the difficulty arises when a once honest man is forced to convince himself.

Nazism, apartheid, religious bigotry, Klu-Kluxery and tainted patriotism flourish in a climate where men begin to believe their own lies. Soon those very lies become institutional maxims and truth shivers in the shadows like a pariah.

Worst of all, however, is when I am deliberately silenced by you. Silence has contributed more to misrule and tyranny than all the lies that have ever been told. If tongues had articulated what the brain knew to be the truth there would be no place for the tyrant or the dictator.

Sometimes courage momentarily wins the day and the brain ordains that the tongue should speak out, but just as the tongue is about to articulate the courageous condemnation the words are halted at the tongue's tip where they languish and fade.

When the foul deed is executed how often have we heard the sideliner say that it was on the tip of his tongue to shout stop but he thought that surely somebody else would say it for him. Give me the lie anytime before a wilful silence, a silence that watches coldly and callously while evil smothers good. Yes, bad as the lie is give it to me before silence.

What a quidnunc you have been. You would be the first to accuse women of having a monopoly on gossip but women are, for the most part, harmless tattlers although there are some who have permanently ruined the innocent as well as the guilty. Women are mere relayers of more outrageous fibs manufactured by man. Even your sainted mother was not above carrying a tale of dubious origins and little substance.

How many innocent holidaying girls are alleged to be absent because of illicit pregnancies and had their characters ruined and their marriage prospects decimated. Did not you yourself add to these defamations without batting an eyelid, more so if the girls in question were of outstanding character. You shamed me then and indeed I would have preferred on such occasions if somebody had cut me off and tossed me to the dogs. You tried to salve your conscience by suggesting that you were only parroting the disclosures of other small-minded men.

How I loathed your silence when your friends were being slandered, but is that not the story of most men's lives? I would have swelled with pride had you invested me with the diction to defend them.

I have no longer any doubt but that men are the harsher and more venomous gossips. Women gossip mostly for the sake of ingratiation but men do it because it's a crime to use a sword but no crime to pierce a heart with the malicious innuendo. Men manufacture. Women distribute.

How I remember the facility with which you broke so many hearts. Oh the gorgeous phrases so sonorous and so mellifluous that flowed from my core as you wooed the greener girls of the countryside! Even I was transported on the run-up to your first conquest, but I quickly grew disillusioned as you trotted out the same base blandishments to female after female.

You scored a bullseye once in every ten throws of the amorous dart. This was good shooting by any standard but how you lied and cheated, always using me to convey the oft-repeated piffle which women seem to lap up like starving cats at a milk basin. They are easily flattered, poor creatures, and they never tire of hearing their praises sung. One day, inevitably, they become hardened after perfidious onslaughts by the likes of you.

When you would hear that a girl's heart was breaking after you tired of her you would quote the sages and say time heals all. I wonder, however, how many of these sages were jilted or betrayed by those they loved. When you fell in love with Lily Lieloly you experienced purity and sanctity and beauty but these were not enough for you. You wanted more, but Lily denied you.

I remember how you brutally defined true love ever after.

"True love," said you with a smirk, "is when a chap wants a girl to hold his hand instead of his population stick."

Glib isn't the world for you. I would sooner you had mouthed the mimesis of a fart. There is much more that I could add but there are other organs anxiously awaiting their turn. Before I conclude I would ask you to use me sparingly when your dander is up. Use me most to forgive and forget and when evil assails you use me not at all.

Sincerely,

Your Tongue.

THE HAIRS OF THE HEAD WRITE

Dear Neighbour,

As we write a white hair falls to the page. It should remind you that you are now in the autumn of your life and that at last you might consider comporting yourself accordingly so as not to embarrass us further.

We who were once black and curly grow thinner and more fragile by the hour. Yet we still manage to compliment each other and how we wish that humans as a whole could do likewise. Here, living together in total harmony, one will notice blacks, browns and yellows, whites and off-whites together with occasional strands of uncommon silver.

At this stage of your life, as seen by others, we present a picture of over-all greyness and this is as it should be having regard for your years, wasted and otherwise. It is about this greyness that we propose to address you. We might dwell upon other aspects of our relationship with you such as the time you shaved your cranium to the very bone after beholding Yul

Brynner in *The King and I* or we might mention the time you dyed us all red or the time you opted for that infernal white splash, but since these were fads we feel that to dwell upon them would be to defeat our real purpose which has to do with the present time and not the past.

Of late we are growing grey for the second time and would like to remain grey this time. The first time was roughly five years ago. We well recall how your long-suffering wife, the once luscious Penelope Fitzfeckid, and your daughters looked on with mounting alarm as the fine white streaks encroached upon the ebony thatch to which they had been accustomed for so long. They imagined, poor feckless creatures, just as Keats's bees imagined that warm days would never cease, that we would never change colour or lose so many of our brotherhood to the passage of time. For our part we were perfectly satisfied. Nature was taking its course. The inevitable was happening. Worse if you were growing bald. Now that would have been calamity! We fear nothing more than approaching baldness. For us baldness means the end of everything.

Back, however, to those females of yours. Of course, you would never give ear when they reminded you that you were consuming too much alcohol or behaving like a lecher or spending too much time with your cronies or not spending enough time at home. Your vanity, the most prickable part of your make-up, was pricked once more. When they subtly suggested to you that the grey might be kept at bay you readily acquiesced and were induced to part with a substantial sum to initiate the first action against what was right and natural.

They purchased for you at a reputable pharmacist's a bottle of Greycure, a mixture which was guaranteed to retain the natural colour of the hair and this by merely using a small quantity of the miraculous composition whenever a grey hair hove into view. Even the cranium itself with whom we are constantly in touch had no objection to our growing grey. Only you, the brain, would disapprove.

You should know by now that a man with a dash of grey in his hair need never grow a moustache or a beard to prove his masculinity. The grey shows that he has been there and back. The white filaments stand out like stripes on a sergeant-major or campaign ribbons on a veteran. This is why most grey-haired young men marry early and successfully and this is why women are so attracted to otherwise ordinary-looking men who have nothing going for them save a touch of grey in the hair.

You should be on your bended knees in thanksgiving that you have greyed with such distinction. Were we hairs but brains we would cherish every last grey rib atop the cranium. Wherever else it may be about the colour grey one thing is absolutely certain: it has an extraordinary effect on females of all ages. We, the hairs, believe that it gives the impression of accomplishment. Certainly the man with a discreet tinge of grey has a head start over his rivals. He doesn't even have to ogle the lady of his fancy. His grey hairs do all the work for him. We also believe that women have infinite trust in grey-haired men. There is a fatherliness about them; they radiate concern. They may be no more than common rogues like yourself but women, more than men, are firm believers in the old legal decree that a grey-haired man is innocent until proven guilty.

Even if all the hair is not grey it would be sufficient if the hirsute area above the auricles were ever so slightly tinged.

When you anointed us with Greycure it worked admirably as far as you were concerned. We were as black as ever we had been and your cronies wondered at the redoubtable napper which defied the years and refused to play host to a single grey hair.

You were a man apart for a while but in the end people grew suspicious. Add to this the fact that a tiny but ominous bald patch made its appearance on your poll. At first this was easily concealed by the deceitful deployment of some of the longer hairs in the patch's vicinity but as time wore on and the bald patch expanded its holding we remaining hairs became painfully aware that it would only be a matter of time before it made an outright bid for monopoly of your entire crown. If anything you became even more panic-stricken than we were and wisely you decided to withhold further applications of the much-vaunted Greycure. It was the wisest move you ever made and ever after when we would hear people say that poor old Tommy Scam hadn't a brain in his head we would bristle as we never bristled before.

While our numbers did not increase there were no

further losses and you vowed to allow nature full rein, sustaining and maintaining your remaining hairs. We have served you well and we have survived the excesses which have done for so many of our immediate colleagues and for greying hairs on every pate all over the world. We feel like parodying old Polonius as he addressed his son Laertes in Hamlet:

"Those hairs thou hast and their adoption tried
grapple them to thy poll with hoops of steel."

I am certain that if Laertes had been allowed to grow older and greyer those would have been the precise words used by his father. The Elizabethans were great warrants to coin the colourful phrase. The father of this day and age would be more likely to say, "Keep your hair on, son."

If you had persevered with the application of the murderous Greycure we have no doubt whatsoever but that your head would now be as bald as the proverbial billiard ball.

It is, we believe, a fine thing to grow bald naturally because all bald men are possessed of shapely, presentable heads which look dignified as well as romantic. However, brains like yourself who forfeit precious ribs through vanity are possessed of mediocre craniums which need considerable camouflage when our artful coverage is withdrawn. What a sorry sight you would be without us. A duck out of water would by infinitely more prepossessing.

We would now like to issue the following statement as an assurance to those who are apprehensive about growing grey and we would expect you to instruct your writing hand that the statement be written in characters clear and submitted to the world through whatever means you may think most effective.

Grey hairs are the harbingers of tolerance and maturity. They complement the lines that come with age and remember too that from a sartorial viewpoint grey goes with everything. For a black head a man needs sprightly feet whereas for a grey head a sensible pace is all that is required. No great feats are expected from the men whose heads we adorn whereas a man with bright colours might be expected to perform feats as colourful as his hair. The old Gaelic poets must take their share of the blame for derogatory attitudes towards grey hairs. When they wrote of men with black hair they compared it to the raven's wing and when they spoke of men with red hair they said it was burnished like the sun. When they spoke of men with fair or blonde hair they said it glistened like gold but when they spoke of men with grey hair they said of them that they were as grey as badgers or as grey as goats.

They should have said as grey as mottled silver or as grey as an evening sky or grey as doves at daybreak or grey as a stand of winter beeches or grey as the Burren of the County Clare or grey as the snowy owl or grey as the Northern Diver. There are a thousand beautiful shades of grey. There is the gentle grey of sea-mist, there is the silvery grey of slates under a full moon and there is oyster grey in the bed of the sea. It's great to be grey when you come to think of it.

For one of the finer tributes paid to us grey hairs we

must look once more to Shakespeare. In the first act of *Julius Caesar* when the conspirators are selecting their henchmen, the requisite characteristics of the various nominees are taken into account. Somebody suggests Cinna the poet and the motion is carried.

"Let us have him," says his nominator, "for his grey hairs."

No more than his grey hairs, mark you. We would also like to make it clear that we male hairs do not expect females to retain their greyness just because we insist upon doing so. For us, however, the retention of our natural grey is the paramount consideration. Even the theatre today has the good sense to realise that black and white are no longer the dominant shades of drama. Greys are now preferable to sheer blacks and whites because unlike these primary colours grey has many shades, each more subtle than the next.

Of all colours we may also presume that grey is the most conciliatory by virtue of the fact that it never obtrudes or dazzles. It has, we believe, a calming quality and we have noted inflammatory situations where the timely arrival of a grey-haired man had the effect of imposing peace and tranquillity upon the warring factions. We who are grey have spoken and, happily, we find ourselves in this time and place presentable, abundant and hopeful that we will never again be subjected to chemical pollution.

Sincerely,

Your Grey Hairs.

THE MEMORY WRITES

Dear Brain,

I recall a votive mass commissioned by your loving mother for the fulfilment of her private intentions. Your father had gone to his grave but six months earlier and if there are choirs of angels in the regions beyond they were surely gathered in their entirety to sing that sainted soul into heaven.

For his likes, heaven if there is one, with its indescribable effulgence and pain-free felicity, was most certainly devised as a just need for his humanitarian activities during his all too short stay in this crucible we call the world.

You were in your late teens and, like all mothers, yours still cherished delusory hopes that you might yet entertain a vocation for the priesthood. The votive candles shimmered in their polished candelabra and no sound save the rustle of the sacred vestments obtruded into that solemn place other than yours and your mother's gentle breathing.

How is it that occasions like these which are designated to impose pious sentiments on the participants very often induce responses which are far from spiritual, responses alas which are the direct opposite of those intended. I am only your memory and cannot choose what you wish to recall. I am a good memory and I store much that is eminently quotable and well worth visual replay, but you prefer to summon up the less savoury aspects of your tainted past.

Instead of praying for your father's soul you permitted your mind to wander to a visit of Connelly's Circus when it had played a matinee in your childhood, and what was it you thought of? The elephants, the lions, the horses and ponies, the juggler, the monkeys? No indeed, oh most lascivious of wretches! Even in the sacred place where you and your mother came to worship you might have been partially forgiven if you had remembered Loco the red-nosed, potbellied clown who had every child under the canvas in stitches.

Earlier that morning I had high hopes for you. Quite unexpectedly and delightfully you recalled glimpses of the snowy summits of the South Kerry mountains in all their pearly whiteness as they strove to survive the warming winds of a bright May morning. There is a godly gleam from mountain snow when the sun assails it. I would have forgiven you if this recollection had persisted throughout the celebration of the holy mass for there is a deep spirituality secreted in the beauties of nature, a spirituality so glorious that God is forever manifesting Himself and his artistry through its magnificent intricacies.

No such lofty pursuits for you, however, who preferred to resurrect the only scene in that particular circus which provoked criticism from the local parish priest, who described it as obscene. That was when Mona Bonelli, the Italian contortionist, wearing a skintight suit, only the skimpiest of briefs and the barest of bras danced on to the centre ring under the spotlight's glare. Her dazzling smile captivated all present but you more than any. Immediately she lifted the hoop through which she would thrust her seemingly boneless body you started to drool and slobber like a starving hound on beholding a string of blushing pork sausages. Granted the girl was sensual and sinuous, even voluptuous when she felt so disposed, but there was a hardness and a craftiness about her which you refused to recognise.

All that concerned you was the way she displayed her shapely body as she twisted and screwed her muscular limbs. There were, I will concede, no angles to her, no warps nor wrinkles nor blemish that could be perceived by the naked eye. With curves she was bountifully endowed and aided by the make-up, the perpetual smile, the shimmering sequins on her scant apparel and the bright spotlights she did succeed in unsettling the less discerning and non-artistic males among the audience.

Long before her performance drew to a close you were completely carried away, and to think that you would preserve this far-off exhibition for the sacred occasion devoted to your father's memory.

I have forgotten the number of times you have recalled Mona Bonelli and countless other scantily clad and unclad visions to induce nocturnal slumber when by the simple expedient of saying your night-time prayers your conscience would just as easily have entrusted you to the waiting arms of Morpheus.

You could not know, of course, poor, weak-willed organ, that the glamorous Mona Bonelli was in reality none other than plain Biddy Muldoon from the county of Waterford and that she was not the nineteen year old titian-haired beauty that she was supposed to be. Rather was she a forty-year-old, mousey-haired, drop-out housewife who had allowed herself some years before to be seduced and latterly taken in tow by the moustachioed ringmaster ˜ Connelly's Circus. Her deserted husband had ever after made it a point to remember the ringmaster in his prayers, day and night, "For," said he to a freshly acquired helpmate, "he has taken the scourge of my life upon himself and heaven will surely be his lot, for he will suffer his hell in this world."

Later that evening, the same Mona Bonelli or Biddy Muldoon was seated in the local hotel where your father had invited you to partake of an orangeade whilst he sampled the excellent potstill whiskey for which the hostelry was renowned. Mona Bonelli, the luscious, titian-haired teenager from the land of the Tiber and the Po was now showing every single one of her forty years and deprived of the glamorous aids of her contortionist's trade she looked a very ordinary creature indeed. You failed to recognise her and even when she vainly tried to ogle your late, lamented father by crossing and uncrossing her still shapely legs you still could not call to mind the body that had transported you such a short while before.

I can never comprehend why you still persist in remembering the more tawdry experiences of your past especially since I carry a large stock of beautiful visions which you would have no trouble remember if only you made the effort. Among other things I have an excellent range of truly beautiful faces including those of your aging mother and your long-suffering spouse and, of course, the innocent faces of your children. I lovingly preserve those of your maiden aunts and benevolent uncles and, dare I mention her name, the lovely Lily Lieloly. No memory could be blamed for cherishing that angelic face.

I have an exciting repertoire of sporting occasions from the lowliest of donkey derbies to the heart-stopping drama of the Aintree Grand National, from your own humble contributions on the playing fields to the dizz heights of the great Olympics. No television set will ever serve you as well as I do and yet you all too often employ me to recall the basest of your activities.

I have a priceless accumulation of sunsets, no two of which are alike and were you to excavate my recesses you would find such an array of wonders treasured over a lifetime that your heart would be permanently uplifted. There are my vaults of cloud formations, cataracts, dawns, twilights, sunbeams and, of course, my seascapes ever ready to reveal themselves.

Remember the blizzards, the cloudbursts and the fuming, raging anger of the oceans. Remember the rolling reverberations of the great thunderstorms, the crackling, the booming and the lingering echoes as the turmoil spent itself in the all-absorbing bosom of the sky. Remember the surging, sweeping floods, their inestimable passion concealed in the sibilant deceptive surges. Oh those rampant, riotous waters, dirging and delving and loamy! I can bring to mind the sounds and the pictures in an instant. Just say the word and I will recall for you the first kiss, the first embrace, the first love of those halcyon days when your heart was unsullied and pure. I have so much that is elevating, so much that will bring you closer to the ideal of self-purification, the only ideal which will truly prepare you for the transition from a known state to an unknown. Prompt me, poise me, nudge me to work for your good. Resist the evil pressures that would have me prostitute my talents so that your unworthy whims might be gratified. Let me resurrect for you the glories and the good deeds, so few in your lifetime to date. Upon recalling these you may go forth and emulate, thus inspiring me to renounce the inglorious and the ignominious.

I will conclude now but before I do I would like to recall for you the most heroic incident which might be credited to you. You were but seven then and you were in the company of an even younger girl who happened to be your playmate of the time. As the two of you passed Drumgooley's farmyard gate, having wandered from a rustic picnic organised by your mother, who should come fussing and flapping from the fowl-run but Drumgooley's gander, a fearsome creature with a nerve-shattering cackle whenever he felt his flock was in danger.

Bravely you ordered your young charge to run for her life while you manfully stood your ground and diverted this bloodthirsty barnyard braggart until she had run clear of danger. Allowing for your age and size this was a monumental feat of bravery, of selflessness, of knight-errantry. It was, however, never to be equalled in the long years that followed, but in recalling it I may perhaps remind you that there was a brief but glorious while when chivalry was your long suit.

Finally I would ask you to use me for the betterment of your immortal soul while conceding that I must also be spiced a little now and then if I am to be entertaining as well as exalting.

Sincerely,

Your Memory.

The Fists Write

Dear Brain,

You have never used us on the face of a woman and for this we partially forgive you. You have never used us on the face of a child and for this we are also ready to partially forgive you. You have never used us on the face, head or body of a man who was down and for this too we partially forgive you. Alas, I cannot forgive you everything, though I wish I could.

I remember the night you smashed to pieces every breakable object in the apartment of your partner in your last *affaires d'amour*. So terrified was that unfortunate creature that she threw herself at your feet and begged you to leave but no! You persisted in pursuing your orgy of destruction which was later to cost you dearly in financial terms for you were obliged to foot the bill in toto for every shred of damage you caused.

Oh poor, foolish, vain fellow! Know you not that affairs are the most shortlived of all relationships. Even a fist knows that. An affair comes like a jet aircraft

71

from the east, dominates the heavens overhead for a few brief moments and then disappears into the western skies and is never seen or heard from again.

An affair is like an air-filled, toy balloon which takes off in all directions at once when its wind is released. It rasps, snorts, squeaks and screeches with a passion and ferocity unbridled, and then flops on the floor a tattered parody of its former self. An affair is a mere sneeze which gathers slowly and disperses quickly. You should have known this and accepted your rejection when your correspondent announced that she had her fill of you and fancied another.

You raised us instantly, your loyal and long-suffering fists, and spent your fury on the inanimate. Battered, bloodied and bruised you thrust us inside your coat and staggered to your home where you didn't even have the common courtesy to lave us with ordinary tapwater or dab us with iodine. We suffered for days on end because of your carelessness.

We will be the first to admit that we are only part-time organs. Sometimes we come and go like lightning, other times like flash floods but alas there are times when you retain our services far above and beyond the call of duty and these are the times when we dislike you most.

It is easy to justify the clenching of a fist as a weapon of defence or as an instrument which might be used to strike a football or a punchbag or indeed for involvement in a fair bout of fisticuffs where the protagonists are willing and able to take each other on.

However, there is a time to unclench, to release, to

forgive and forget and to carry on with the business of living and this is where you frequently failed us, for you would not instruct your heart to relent.

So it was that we were unwillingly retained when we might have been peacefully broken up into our many components. Being part-time organs provides us with many compensations so long as you, the proprietor, use us as part-time employees.

When your anger goes we go. In fact we need never exist if you were not so quick to react, if you were not so easily incited, so readily influenced for all the wrong reasons.

We fists are often petrified and activated for reasons of which we rarely approve and if you were to ask the average fist why it is so clenched and why its knuckles show so white, that fist would shake its figurative head in sorrow and frustration and then hang it in shame. We know because we are fists and a fist is not an instrument of affection or love. It does not lie down with peace and harmony. It is hard and hurtful and the longer it remains in this state the less good it bodes for those whom it may encounter. It has little discernment while it remains closed and often all and sundry can fall foul of it with disastrous consequences for its victims and proprietor.

Please remember that ninety-nine times out of a hundred there is no need of us even though you may think otherwise. You, the brain, are solely responsible for our inhumanity, our obstinacy, our inflexibility and only you, the brain, can soften and subdue us.

There are happy days, weeks, even months when we

are non-existent. Our various parts fill other useful roles while we are dormant. Then, unfortunately, as a result of a chance remark, an allegedly unkind cut, a ridiculous, meaningless slight, we are mobilised once more and alerted for destruction even though it is a mobilisation that all too often backfires, leaving you with a bloody nose and broken fingers.

We will now, before concluding, pose you a few questions. Have you ever seen a clenched fist in the company of a laugh? Have you ever seen a fist being clenched while its owner rendered a lovesong? Have you ever seen a man with clenched fists embracing a woman? Have you ever heard of a man who made love with clenched fists or a man who stroked a girl's hair with his fist? Of course not, for the good reason that a fist only does injury whereas the actions to which I have referred call for softness and tenderness.

The only really good thing about us is that when your anger subsides we are dissolved. Now that the years are creeping up on you I think it is high time you retired us altogether. Dismiss us for once and for all and show the world that you have come to terms with yourself and the people about you. Grey hairs and clenched fists seem to us the most unseemly of companions. Wrinkles and clenched fists look even more ridiculous. Retire us at once, in God's name, before you make a complete fool of yourself!

Sincerely,

Your Fists.

THE PENIS WRITES

Dear Master,

I write to you as the most reviled of all your organs, objurgated and calumniated since the inception of copulation and constantly blamed for misdeeds which I freely admit to perpetrating – but always on your instructions. Anything I have ever done has been instigated by you.

There I would be pendant and somnolent, and occasionally out of commission, when suddenly you would shout "tenshun!" and I would be obliged to spring instantly into action.

I was ever ready because eternal vigilance was my motto since I first became aware of your extraordinary and ungovernable proclivity towards the opposite sex.

Now that you have moved on into the years one would expect a katabasis or some slight contraction in the carnal drive. If anything, alas! you would seem to be more inclined than ever before towards sexual debauchery and would motivate me around the clock if you could bring yourself to stay awake that long.

God grant a silver bed in Heaven to your sainted, paternal grandmother; it was she who said that the body should be seven days dead before the penis would fully subside and even then she contended there were isolated cases where this much-maligned organ was seen to be still the outstanding feature in resurrected cadavers which had been interred months before. If this is true the cadaver was no cadaver. Rather was it a body in a state of suspended animation. An old wives' tale I dare say but it shows that no female in her right mind would ever place the least trust, dead or alive, in the organ of organs, as I once heard it called by the captious old midwife who first brought you into the world.

It was she who said that ninety-nine out of every hundred males should be castrated at birth and the one percent isolated but sumptuously cosseted solely for the purpose of perpetuating the human species, "For," said she, "of all the attachments of the trunk it is the one which is to be trusted least."

How wrongfully labelled have we penises always been. The old woman, for all her knowledge of the world, should have laid the blame for all my exploits fairly and squarely at your door.

I once heard an itinerant evangelist suggest at a street corner in the city of Dublin that there was nothing so profound as a common erection.

The truth is that there is nothing less profound for the pump in question, the pump of life, is the most uncomplicated adjunct of the entire human system, so whenever we hear a person say that he or she has read or heard something profound what it really means is that they are more mystified after experiencing this so-called profundity than they were before.

The point I would ram home – you'll find the expression endearing I'm sure! – is that I am simply your puppet and that I have no influence whatsoever over my destiny.

There are people who say that excessive drinking brings out the worst in me. What they should be saying is that it bring out the worst in you and that you are capable of submitting me to the most extreme excesses after a sustained bout of intemperance. You would place my very existence in jeopardy such is your lack of restraint and distortion of outlook after an alcoholic shaughraun.

You take the whip to conscience and oust him from his watchtower whenever it suits your vile purpose.

Conscience, poor creature, is a head-shaker and a tut-tutter rather than a dictator. It is you who dictates to and manipulates poor Mister Conscience until he is more of a yes-man than an honest witness for that which prosecutes on behalf of the Creator.

I remember just before your first fall cut you irretrievably adrift from lovely Lily Lieloly, you were at that manky stage in your debauch-filled career when a choice had to be made between your continuing virginity and your likely defilement.

I had fondly hoped that because Lily Lieloly was also a virgin you would preserve me for that glorious union when you and Lily would consummate your betrothal and bring everlasting joy to both your hearts.

Virginity is, unfortunately, something of a souvenir, often priceless to its owner but frequently worthless on the open market.

You held yours in so little regard that you unashamedly and heedlessly disposed of it at the first available opportunity. Even after that first disappointing encounter I had hoped that your unsatisfactory initiation into the sorry rite of illicit deflowering would signal your return to the road of righteousness.

It was not to be and in no time at all you had exhausted the last reserves of local harlots and accommodating amateurs. Soon you were to become a familiar figure in the iniquitous dens of nearby cities until you were rendered temporarily *hors de combat* by a four-feet-eleven masseuse who, for a few extra quid, provided you with what she termed the full treatment as advertised in the jargon of the trade, on a charge sheet which hung between framed photographs of the late John F. Kennedy and Pope John the twenty-third.

It was Sir Alexander Fleming, through the medium of his miraculous penicillin, who must be praised and thanked for your speedy recovery. You were to indulge your weakness at colossal expense of both the physical and financial kind before finally succumbing to the wiles and monies of the oldish and plainish heiress, Miss Penelope Fitzfeckid.

There followed several years of marital harmony, during which time Penelope presented you with two daughters and a bouncing boy.

Then one day you called me up unexpectedly for

active service far from the home front. It was the evening of some rugby international at Twickenham.

There you were one minute carousing and chorusing with your cronies and the next in the rear seat of a taxi heading for one of those haunts where you once excelled yourself, or so you believed, in those rakish days before marriage.

You were recognised at once and rapturously received by the never-ageing Madame who, according to herself, had spent the intervening years wondering and worrying about your sustained exile from her buxom charges, all of who had now been replaced by younger and more agile exponents of the high and ancient art of copulation.

There were times during that long week-end when I feared for our survival but miraculously you managed to escape visitation from the wide variety of painful diseases which were then rampant in that particular parlour.

We were not to be so lucky on a later occasion which I will also never forget for another reason, this being that you put me to work when I was no longer capable and made me the butt of your paramour's vulgar wit – and not one word in defence out of you to whom I have given decades of incomparable service. Instead you laughed loud and long.

You once remarked to a crony that I had betrayed you. Your exact words were:

"I might have been a chap of infinite morality, a veritable paragon had I not been let down by the most contumacious pudenda!"

I heard you announce another time, in an effort to justify a shortlived affair with a local matron:

"What a wonderful fellow I would be but for this baggage of reproduction which demoralises my every thought and deed."

Who knows better than yourself, my dear master, that it was nothing but your own interfemoral phantasising which was the paramount contribution in all our efforts. It has been said that I have no conscience and for once they speak the truth about me, for it is you who possesses the conscience and I can take some satisfaction from the fact that it keeps you awake nights.

However, it is true to say that your conscience takes leave of absence whenever I am called upon to illicitly execute your iniquitous behests. Afterwards, when your conscience returns, I am sickened by the excess remorse in which you wallow, remorse, I might add, of little duration.

I will not cite other acts which I was obliged to perform on your behalf but I must mention your habit of urinating into your shoes whilst in your cups and indeed leaving your bed after a night consuming gallons of beer and advancing to the head of the stairs where you would set a minor cascade into motion. There must have been at least a hundred bed-wettings after your beer sessions. Indeed in your drunken stupors you have peed into purses, flower pots, frying pans, pianos and wastepaper baskets, everywhere in fact but into the numerous chamber pots which your long-suffering spouse would so thoughtfully and strategically arrange at the precise places where you had emptied yourself before.

Often on your way home from pub crawls you would do it against dustbins and doorways, telephone and electricity poles, shop windows and sacrosanct monuments. No place was sacred when the urge beset you. Worst of all was that pre-wedding night when by some perverted mischance you located your mother's wedding bonnet and filled its upturned crown with a froth-covered outflow which would have done justice to a Shergar or a Nijinsky!

There was a time you did it through the keyhole of a watchful neighbour and very nearly deprived the poor creature of a vision already impaired from exposure to constant draughts and rain-squalls. There was the time you attempted to do it against the trousers of a custodian of the peace and had to exert all your influences to keep the matter out of the courts.

I will never forget the night you were caught red-handed doing it into a flower pot in the window of the local bully boy. The kick which he implanted fairly and squarely on me and the remainder of your apparatus left me unwell for days. I have often asked myself how is it that man will persist in aiming knees, boots and fists at that part of the anatomy which has given him the most pleasure. It is one of the more intriguing aspects of man's mental infirmity.

If I were asked to recall the most outrageous statement you ever made I would suggest that it was that which referred to me as follows:

"A man with an enthusiastic penis," you said, "is the

servant of a headstrong master!"

One of your cronies insisted that you deserved the title of philosopher after such a perceptive declaration whereas if the truth were told it was about as philosophical an inanity as the nocturnal braying of a wandering jackass. Too well you know that I was never your master. You and you alone are responsible for my every action and my survival for when you go I will have to go with you, and when you decay I will decay too. But for the miracle of penicillin I would have long since capitulated to the overpowering influences of your many silent and most unwelcome visitors, chief amongst whom are those age-old invaders – clap, syphilis and pox. Monday morning blues was your way of referring to the first of this terrible trio, and what a brave face you would put on when you would whisper to the discreet apothecary in his dispensary that you required a small jar of mercurial ointment often so unpharmaceutically referred to by the loathsome name of "blue butter". I refuse to recall the occasions and the wenches responsible for these visitations for I would not have it on my conscience that I scandalised the gentle reader with the more lurid details of your awesome sex life.

I am at a loss as to how I should conclude. Should I beg you to moderate your lifestyle, make representations to your better nature or ask you to turn to religion as a safeguard against eternal damnation? It would not matter one whit how I might address you since, as far as I am concerned, you have always seen to it that I will remain the most capricious of organs so that no trust whatsoever may be reposed in poor me!

Faithfully,

Your Penis.

THE NOSE WRITES

Dear Brain,

The only thing I can really say in your favour is that you never deliberately altered me. Altered I was by your headstrong foolishness. Would you had heeded the sage advice of the forgotten poet who wrote so wisely:

Those who in quarrels interpose
Must often wipe a bloody nose.

I recall that night in Forty-Second Street when you announced in a topless bar that Richard Nixon was a gentleman. If memory serves me correctly you described him as the most misunderstood man in America.

I'll concede that you had no appraisal whatsoever of the coming blow but you might more profitably have kept your mouth shut especially since you were both inebriated and outnumbered. I was well and truly broken by the outsize fist of a squat Puerto Rican with no neck. Earlier you had told him in your own inimitable and cavalier way that he reminded you of John the Baptist with his head glued back on rather artlessly.

It was one of your more suicidal statements. However, we soon put all that behind us and after a botchy repair job by one of New York's most expensive quacks I was still a fairly prepossessing proboscis.

Then there was the time you all but exterminated yourself drinking whiskey. Your liver, however, is better qualified to speak about your whiskey period than I am but I must remind you, in case of a recurrence, that I doubled in size during that time and my colour was temporarily transformed from a natural pink to a vile puce.

But for the nasal sentiments of Cyrano de Bergerac so passionately and eloquently conveyed I must surely have become clogged and inoperable. Oh that was a great declamation!

"Let me inform you that I am proud of such an appendage since a big nose is the proper sign of a friendly, good, courteous, witty, liberal and brave man."

When your doctor issued his ultimatum that your wife's widowhood was imminent unless you refrained at once from imbibing rotgut, you turned to beer. My size and hue were restored within weeks and tragedy was narrowly averted.

Apart from playing host to mucousness, liquid and congealed, I am also the harbourer of your sixth sense. You might say that we are one. I do not expect gratitude. It is part of my job to see to your survival and this is why I nurture and cosset this most valuable of all the senses although I will never know why such a lowly organ as I was chosen to be the repository of one so gifted.

I myself have no difficulty in smelling smoke, fumes and gases provided you are not drugged with alcohol but the sixth sense which I house is a smeller of pitfalls; just as I direct you towards appetising food so does the sixth sense upon smelling trouble direct you in the opposite direction.

The sixth sense is capable of detecting the approach of gracious in-laws and mendicant relations. The sixth sense, often confused with experience, determines from the volume and tempo of a simple knock on a door whether joy or sorrow wishes to be admitted. The housing and maintenance of this priceless instinct is a most onerous responsibility and were I a boastful, trumpeting nose I should be blowing my coals all day long.

Vanity is not my long suit but I will tell you this for I know it to be Gospel. When you first met Lily Lieloly she did not look into your eyes nor at the ebony curls atop your young and imprudent head. She did not gasp as others did at the whiteness and uniformity of your dazzling teeth nor did she judge you by the manliness of your unwrinkled brow. No sir! She looked at me, your nose, the only truly classical feature of an otherwise lacklustre face. She looked at me and that look lingered longer than any look I have ever experienced before or since. Her full lips parted as though she would speak. No words came but I sensed that if she had spoken she would have said:

"Thou art the noblest Roman of them all."

There was that awful period when you sported the moustache. You imagined you were being trendy whereas, in fact, all you did was to make yourself look ridiculous. Growing a moustache next to a nose is like pouring patented, bottled sauce over the mouth-watering creation of a world-class chef. I can stand on my own. The day you shaved off that bristling horror girls began to look at you again, particularly at that part of your dial where I hold sway.

There was the time you had your handkerchiefs monogrammed. The subsequent damage to my tender tissue has not yet healed from the blowing you gave me. Every time you wanted to show off you whipped out that crudely-labelled cotton duster and trumpeted like a rogue elephant, so that all could hear and, hearing, take notice of your scribble-defiled snot-rag. You must never use me in that fashion again. I am attached to your face for the primary purpose of taking pressure off you. Granted I assist with your breathing but your mouth is big enough to cope amply with that. It is a good job that the same mouth forms such a substantial gulf between myself and the jaw which receives most of the credit for being the gritty, gutsy hardchaw of the face whereas I am extended far beyond his utmost extremity and I am bloodied a hundred times more often than he is fractured or broken, bloodied so often by the probing nails of your index fingers as they scout my interior for recalcitrant snots that it's a wonder I'm not whittled away altogether.

I can never understand why I should be picked and eviscerated by unwelcome fingers, especially when I don't need picking. A high-quality, white, linen handkerchief discreetly and effectively used without resorting to excess is all that's required to see that my passageways are kept open. I am otherwise well able to maintain myself. Desist, therefore, from this vile practice before a nail-induced haemorrhage bleeds you to death.

You might also refrain from cocking your nose at people who are worse off materially than you are. I was created for better things. How often am I reminded of Dean Swift as you proceed upon your shallow pontifications about subjects where your ignorance is total.

How haughtily he cocks his nose
To tell what every schoolboy knows.

This is you down to the ground. Always remember that I am never haughty but that I am always noble. Please try to see further than me from now on. I am the most modest of appendages and I need not be. Three times in one short passage in *Romeo and Juliet*, the world's greatest tragedy, there is reference to me:

"Oh! then I see Queen Mab hath been with you....
She is the fairies' midwife and she comes
In shape no bigger than an agate stone
On the forefinger of an alderman
Drawn by a team of little atomies
Athwart men's noses as they lie abed....
Sometimes she gallops o'er a courtier's nose
And sometimes comes she with a tithe-pig's tail

Tickling a parson's nose as he lies asleep.
Then dreams he of another benefice."

So you see, my friend, you are not being addressed by a common protuberance and if you must pick me make sure your nails are clean.

Finally, I would ask you to impose a more even tone over my snoring and try to avoid those fretful, fitful snorts that make for staggered snores which are anathema to me. An aborted snore is the most frustrating experience which may befall a nose. There is nothing a nose likes better than being snored through and I am no exception. Also, God bless me, I enjoy the occasional sneeze.

Sincerely,

Your Nose.

THE HEART WRITES

My dear Brain,

You had better listen to me because for all your mastery of all the organs you cannot be aware of the number of beats which are left to me. I myself have a pretty fair idea but you give the impression you don't care.

You could, I dare say, devise a computer which when provided with the speed, strength and regularity of my thumping in relation to other complex factors would provide you with a rough idea of my maximum beat capacity.

The truth is, however, that while I may have a rough idea of the number left I could be utterly wrong as so many other hearts have been in the past. Even specialists with brains superior to yours have been caught out repeatedly.

I am, of course, one with your soul which we are told is immortal. I am sure the soul exists and so are you. The soul it is which waits patiently for the end when it will assume our spiritual remains into itself for the flight to the hereafter and to God knows what. How's that Anne Hathaway's husband puts it?

For in that sleep of death, what dreams may come
When we have shuffled off this mortal coil
Must give us pause!

Pause is right, and if we were pausing all our days and doing nought other than pausing on this particular theme we would be as wise before as after. Therefore live, dear brain, revere the day and the night you live in for it is all you may comprehend, and mark out a decent place in that land of no return by being decent here. Let us hear from Anne Hathaway's husband again:

The undiscovered country from whose bourne
No traveller returns, puzzles the will.

Puzzles the will indeed, and will puzzle it until I cease beating. Therefore, be about your business for puzzlement begets fuddlement and your puniness, poor limited creature, might only be shown to be more pronounced.

We are as incapable of understanding God's designs for us and the concept of life after death as the beasts of the field are of comprehending the quantum theory of radiation. Indeed you would probably achieve a better result by putting a common jackass solely in charge of a human heart-transplant than assembling the world's finest brains to solve the mystery of the hereafter.

The moral here is to know your limitations and have faith in your present state, and trust in the creator's plans for you. Trust in God and find peace of mind. How simple for those who can comply.

Alas, the imagination which you excite and ferment beyond its normal capacity complies with little save that in which it may indulge itself. I am your most faithful friend. I will be with you to the last when your soul will transport us to that realm which is beyond our ken.

How often, you ignoble wretch, have you implied in the everlasting tavern-wrangle which is the ultimate in human confusion, that there is no creator, no God, nothing at the end of all.

Like all alcoholically-stupified brains you speak as though you had inside knowledge, as though you had just heard direct from the creator. I believe that God is omnipotent but sometimes I must be forgiven if I suspect that He is a little deaf, for if He heard only a little of the diabolical criticism to which He is subjected in public houses He would terminate the existence of the inane morons who flagellate Him.

Maybe I'm wrong and maybe it is how you provide Him with the laughter which is echoed in his thunder.

"There is no God!" I once heard you insist in a public house in Galway after your four kings were well and truly demolished by a straight flush of dubious origins in the biggest pot of the night. If you had kept your eyes open and watched the dealer you would only have had to contend with a very ordinary flush but you were too busy calling the barman's attention to your empty glass.

You doubt the hereafter and yet you instruct the

ever-baffled mouth to pray for your deceased fore-
bears, and with your equally confused hands you disburse mass offerings for their eventual exit from
purgatory and entry into the heaven in which you
place no credence while sojourning on earth.

Sometimes it is as difficult for me to understand you
as it is for you to understand the hereafter. It would
seem that you endorse heaven with part of you and
dismiss it with another. In your interminable tavern-
agonising, fortified by overdoses of whiskey, you dismiss God's very existence and yet you pray in the dark
or in times of trial for the same God's protection and
forgiveness.

Your petty theological rantings have the same effect
on God as the droppings of an underfed insect on the
water level of the Grand Coulee Dam.

How well I remember the countless times you would
scoff at the idea that in the hereafter there would be
an immediate judgement, where every last sin, venial
and mortal, would be paraded before you, before God
and before all the angels and saints and before all the
happy souls who were granted access to the sight of
God by virtue of their propensity towards good during
their stay here.

"How for Christ's sake," you would ask, "could anybody be aware of every last deed and every last
thought of every last person who quits this mortal turmoil?"

It's a wonder you weren't rendered totally deaf by
God's laughter, you heretical nonentity.

"How could any so-called divinity," you went on, to

the wonder and delight of your befuddled cronies, "be capable of remembering the countless repetitive transgressions so wearisome and so inconsequential that they should really count for nothing at all, and at the same time seem incapable of acknowledging cataclysmic occurances where millions die?

"How does He manage to keep a mental record," you queried further, "of every impure thought to assail the minds of honest men and women?"

The answer is simple, you poor benighted heathen. It is no strain whatsoever on God with His omniscient brain to store a record of all man's words, thoughts and deeds down to the most infinitesimal iota, from the beginning to the end of time. It is a God who provided man with the brain that devises computers which will one day soon be capable of revealing all of the world's knowledge and all of man's doings at the press of a button. Imagine the immensity of a brain which in its stride creates thousands of brains like yours every single day as a matter of course, and this among a million other wonderful creations among all the universes and galaxies ad infinitum.

You talk of cataclysmic happenings. Nature is God's brainchild just as man is, and He has given both the power to create and destroy at will thereby justly absolving himself but nevertheless dutifully recording all.

Alas, man's control of both himself and nature is limited in one vital respect. God has seen to that lest man endeavour to destroy God and thus destroy himself. That is God's charity at work and charity is the material which I house on your behalf together with love and compassion, beauty, truth and tenderness which temper the savagery that often runs berserk in you.

Only I, the heart, am capable of anointing you with love so that you do not instruct your limbs to run amuck on murderous rampages.

Alas, I am powerless when your sensitive cess, fibres, layers and ineffable what-have-you are shocked and shattered by pressures and accidents, by traumas and tragedies.

Then I bleed for you as do the hearts of good folk everywhere. Here all truly human hearts extend themselves. Here they brim with concern.

So far you have escaped any serious damage which is truly miraculous when your alcoholic intake and propensity to disaster are taken into account. It is a miracle how your hundreds of all too impressionable components, from the central canal to the pyramidal tract, have withstood the sustained barrage to which you have subjected them since you first learned how to walk.

As far as our relationship goes I am always here supporting you, ever ready to heal and succour to the best of my ability, unendingly repaired to invoke all my human features so that they might operate for your benefit and for your salvation. Yet most of the time you take me for granted, except on those rare occasions when, through your self-indulgence, you force me to beat irregularly and even make me pause for breath or miss a beat on my perilous travail.

My workload is mighty but you never accord me a particle of the credit I deserve and yet in the body of Christ I am the sacred centrepiece, the well of compassion, the only divine dimension.

A million songs have been written about me. The loveliest and most everlasting of melodies have been composed on my behalf. Multitudes of jingles and rhymes are addressed to me every day. Wordsworth was only one of a hundred immortals who singled me out for particular mention:

Thanks to the human heart by which we live
Thanks for its tenderness, its joys and fears.

And what does elegant Tennyson say:

'Tis only noble to be good
Kind hearts are more than coronets.

And how does humble Shadwell say it?

Words may be false and full of art
Sighs are the natural language of the heart.

And poor, great Goldsmith:

For other aims his heart had learned to prize
More skilled to raise the wretched than to rise.

All poets great and small have celebrated with me. When lesser organs and weary limbs clamour for the bugle of the brain to sound the retreat it is I who stands fast and bears the brunt. It is my courage that sees the body through. I am the rallier, the core. I have no boundaries. I am fathomless in my fearlessness, infinite in my mercy.

Even when you are transmitting demented demands for parley or submission I stand firm. I am the last redoubt. In the final analysis you are not the worst of brains, although by no means are you the best.

I give you some hope, however, out of my love for you. Let there be one good deed, one really unselfish act, one major contribution to the idea of goodness to show you possess the potential for a future which will be the opposite to your past. If this honest recital seems to you to be emotional and maudlin please to remember that it is.

From,

The Heart.

THE RIGHT EAR WRITES

Dear Brain,

Please pay attention to your right ear. My comrade at the other side of the face wishes me to address you on its behalf as well. Indeed it would do so itself but for the fact that you once forgot to duck in a bar-room punch-up, resulting from a political imbroglio, and subjected it to the full impact of an outsize fist swung in the widest possible of arcs from the floor upwards, arriving ultimately with ever-increasing force dead smack on target and utterly destroying the entire area of that pitiful organ from helix to lobule.

Medical treatment, as the song said, failed o'er and o'er. The utricle and the auricle and the epitympanic recess, as well as the tympanic membrane and several other areas of its interior, were totally destroyed. It is now labelled a cauliflower and this it must remain until your time and ours draws to a close.

I believe I have served you well. Everything and anything from the lowliest buzz to the loftiest whine has been conveyed to you unerringly. Every message has been delivered. There is nothing within the range of human earshot that I have not faithfully conveyed to you, much of it distressfully and much of it joyfully, distressfully as when I conveyed news of your father's demise to you having been informed of the tragedy on your behalf by your tearful mother.

Perhaps the most moving and tenderest communication which I ever picked up was that which was delivered by your father when you were a wild young fellow. How's that Ledwidge puts it:

When will was all the Delphi you would heed,

Lost like a wind within a summer wood.

How well your father understood you. Of course, we must not forget that in his heart he was always young. He understood youth and he endeavoured all his life, as in your case, to cultivate it and cherish it.

How fondly I remember his mellifluous voice, never raised in anger but ever pleading, restrained and paternally sweet to me whose joyous task it was to deliver his lofty sentiments and sage advice tempered with good humour to your often inattentive self.

If you had received even one quarter of the warnings I transmitted to you you would be twice the man you are today. Oh the pearls of wisdom, the incomparably shrewd observations and the noble precepts which your father would have you treasure and which I handled with velvet gloves as I presented them to you. I believe, of all the sounds I processed, the dearest to me were your father's pronouncements.

The low, lapping sound of river water was another

joy. So, too, was the loving whisper of a tender maid as was the monotone of the salt sea on a calm day. So too was sweet birdsong and the plaintive skirl of distant bagpipes, and how I loved the chiming of evening bells made heavenly by the holy singing of cloistered monks. I loved, too, the laughter of boys and girls, the rich, rare voices of mellow women, the far-off baying of hounds in the late watches, your mother's tender summons when you strayed by. And oh! the awful sorrow when I called you from sleep on her behalf to tell you that he had passed on before his time.

Of all the messages I was ever obliged to deliver that was the one I liked least. Even when your father was silent in your company it was a silence that emphasised his presence. His quiet breathings were like benedictions upon me and armed only with tranquillity he always imposed a balm on your troubled spirit. He knew when to speak and when not. Oh for those deep silences that only I can appreciate. True silence is no accident. It has to be created slowly. Hopkins was one of your father's great favourites:

Elected silence, sing to me

And beat upon my whorled ear.

If I could only choose the sounds I wished to hear, but I am subject and must acknowledge ever the feeblest whisper, the faintest sigh, the lowliest croak, the most savage roar, the most rending tumult, the drums, the brasses and the deafening clamour. All must be received and converted by my complex apparati with the maximum accuracy and dispatched with pure articulation.

When a man says his hearing is deceiving him the

ear must look to its machinery for, more often than not, omniparous nature must see to my needs. You never think about me. Always you take me for granted. Where would you be if I were cut off or damaged beyond repair because of your negligence! But let us return to your father and his rich humours. He put it well, God rest his impeccable soul, when he said that the heart had only so many beats.

A particular heart, of course, may exceed its allotted number through stimulation or suspension but, by and large, all hearts have fixed limitations.

I will recall, as you do, how your father called you aside one haze summer's afternoon and invited you to take a seat in the small garden, sweetened, at the time, with the scents of herbs and flowers.

As a prelude to what he was about to convey to you he cleaned out the bowl of his pipe and began to pare paper-thin slivers from the plug of Bendigo tobacco which he had extracted from his waistcoat pocket.

Having pared a sufficiency he placed it in the palm of his left hand and ground it patiently with the base of his right until he brought it to the required consistency.

Those soft almost inaudible sounds were to me what honey is to the taste buds, what a girl's waist is to the lusty youth. How this simple paternal exercise of pipe-filling always fascinated you. I recall how he gently stuffed the pipe bowl with the shredded plug before thrusting the stem into his mouth. Then came the moment of fruition when he lighted the match which ignited the tobacco. Upwards spiralled the blue, fragrant smoke to be scudded and blown westwards before the temperate summer wind. It was a ritual which he used most of his life to impose a calming influence on delicate situations and the situation as it existed between you and he at that time was delicate in the extreme.

It was not long after the fateful evening when you substituted the local baggage for the lovely Lily Lieloly. After the baggage had come a sequence of similar involvements until you became so immersed in fornication that a concerned neighbour of the female gender felt constrained to put your most virtuous mother in the picture.

So horrified was that gracious lady by the inklings revealed that she could not lower herself to confront you. Your father, filling the role played by so many fathers from time immemorial, opened by informing you that it was not his intention to sermonize or condemn and mumbled in jumbled asides how well he understood such matters as the heyday in the blood and the sowing of wild oats and all that! Then he came to the point poor man.

"Tommy," said he most paternally, "it has come to my attention that you have been engaged in questionable pursuits with undesirable females. It saddens my heart to hear this and indeed your poor mother's heart is on the verge of breaking."

You had the grace to bend your head and avert your furiously blushing face. It was then that your father, in his wisdom, rose to the occasion.

"The heart which beats in your young breast,

Tommy," he went on, "has only so many beats and these beats increase in speed and volume whenever man allows himself to indulge in unchaste thoughts about the opposite sex. If mere thinking causes this acceleration of the human heart, what dizzy speeds are generated by physical contact with a buxom damsel of tartish disposition?"

He paused at his stage, if memory serves me correctly, and savoured a deep pull on his pipe. Instantly the tobacco in the bowl glowed red. Smoke issued from between the teeth at either side of the pipe-stem and from the now florid bowl several gossamer-thin trails of smoke were wafted upwards to breezy disintegration. Estimating that sufficient time had passed for his sentiments to sink in he resumed.

"Bad as physical contact such as kissing and embracing undoubtedly are," said he solemnly, "there is no known method of recording the astronomical velocity created by that most demanding and murderous act commonly known as copulation. Whilst even in moderation this heady exercise has been known to cause total physical collapse and subsequent mental derangement, can you imagine the risk to which a young and undeveloped heart is subjected when its equally immature proprietor exercises no restraint whatsoever, but actually persists consistently with this suicidal practise until the heart is left without a single beat and there lies a ghastly corpse where once stood a handsome young man."

Here your beloved father ended his loving admonition. Would that you had taken in his words. You cried salt tears when he had finished and vowed there and then to tread the straight and narrow.

In less than a week you were tripping the troublous trail of debauch once more, you father's words instantly forgotten the moment your senses were assailed by the perfumed swish of a prodigal skirt.

Would that you had one-twentieth the concern for your health that your father had. I might not now be counting your beats, wondering where the next one is coming from and fearful that there might not be a next one at all! I always listen apprehensively to that wayward heart of yours but you are what you are and I am only an ear, a servant as faithful as any but with infirmity beckoning more imperiously as time goes by.

Faithfully yours,

The Right Ear.

REAR APERTURE WRITES

Dear Master,

No doubt you will be surprised to hear from me. I have unsuccessfully tried every other means of communication at my disposal. These are very often unacceptable to those who may avail themselves of orthodox means.

Up until this time, because of my extreme situation, I have had no choice but to express myself after the frowned-upon fashion of rear apertures everywhere. Few willingly listen to our protestations.

At the outset I must ask you to forgive the audacity of such a rotten stinker as I and to make allowance for my squalorous background and my undeserved reputation for underhand practices.

Do not, I implore you, be put off by my suspect address. Remember that many have achieved greatness in spite of their lowly origins. I know you love me the least of all your dominions and who, in truth, could love me for myself alone whose chief role is to channel the body's waste from its putrid confines to the world outside, a world visible to me only once in a blue moon when you are in dire need of a toilet in the great outdoors.

My secondary task is to convey and release the audible and inaudible, the fetid and the odourless gases of the dark interior. Sounds easy, but as one of your American cousins was once heard to remark:

"Try being an asshole the day after Saint Patrick's Day and see how you like it!"

Sometimes the anus is suddenly pressurised. I am not warned in advance and there is a foul-up. Nobody likes me for this although I am not to blame. Which of us has not endured this unhappy and embarrassing experience at least once in a lifetime!

It is I who refines and renders articulate all the explosive protestations of the anus. I am the ultimate processor of every sound that is allowed to escape from the behind. Only for me the disgusting bombast of these unsavoury revelations would be unbearably raucous.

It is I who conditions and musicalises these uncouth outbursts till they are often no more than prolonged plaints, inoffensive and sometimes amusing to the surprised listener.

Now and then there are renegades who surprise the system and who shock and confuse those of sensitive backgrounds who may happen to be in the vicinity, thus ensuring that my rating stays at zero. I can accept this. You might say I've grown up with it. What I cannot accept is the contemptible way you treat me, the absence of any sort of regard for my feelings, the never-ending workload, your insanitary attitude, your verminous, unwashed, pathogenic underclothes, your germ-infested, unsterilised hands, your recklessness in choice of toilets, most notably the unflushed and obviously contaminated, where you will persist in irresponsibly depositing your buttocks for long periods while you futilely endeavour to make up your mind whether you are going to perform or not.

This is a most frustrating time for me. There I am, exposed to my natural enemies, willing and able to assist you in the discharge of your internal wastes while you persist with fitful piddling and misdirected pondering.

May God preserve rear apertures everywhere from the pensive and the pondering. Of all the scourges I have endured and in their entirety they would fill a book, the brooking defecator is easily the most despicable. He is a martyr to his own abstraction. He completely dispels from his mind the purpose which first brought him to the WC and indulges in wide-ranging flights of long-lasting fancy while the unprotected aperture is prey to the thousand contaminations for which privvies are justly noted.

The longer I am allowed to remain exposed the greater the risk of infection and the less likelihood of any form of comprehensive cacation whereas with truly marathon sittings there is often the likelihood of no motion at all.

From my obstructed position I have no way of ascertaining what sort of expression dominates your visage during these extended sits and squats, whether it be rapture or sorrow, common contentment or simple suspension.

I dare say you might call me the blind eye of the anatomy but then anything is better than being called an asshole day in, day out. I suspect that while you sit fallow and functionless there is imposed upon your lineaments a trance-like expression which brooks neither interference or distraction.

You are at peace with yourself and the world and this is essential for man's well-being as long as it's not overdone. I have listened often while you rendered tedious soliloquies concerning your past, your present and the life of the world to come.

The real tragedy arises when you go on and on until you are so exhausted that the primary purpose of your visit has been supplanted by some other goal.

Fine if you submitted me to exposure in the open countryside where the air is pure and there is no likelihood of infection. This happens so rarely, however, that the experience might well be described as the annual holiday of the down-under cavity. Even when you do submit me to the benign influences of the rustic scene you are in such an almighty hurry that my holiday is over before it even starts.

When you fall asleep in the indoor toilet my nightmare begins for by so doing you extend an open invitation to every circumjacent creepy-crawley and parasite besides announcing to long-despairing germs that the time has at last come when they may assume bellicose roles once more.

The seismograph of my sensitive perimeter records the most shattering, devastating agitation while you are transported to the world of dreams forgetting the fearful dangers to which we are both exposed.

I recall with total horror the times you fell asleep on the seats of stinking WCs. I would listen to your drunken snoring while assorted insects mobilised themselves in lesser keys, using my vulnerable surrounds as landing bases for the later perpetration of outrages I dare not mention. Often you would sleep for hours, your grinding, grating snorts and intemperate skirls, oblivious to the frenzied pounding upon the privy door by legitimate aspirants to the vitreous throne which you so callously usurped.

Who could blame one of these demented claimants for wanting to implant the toe of a stout boot fairly and squarely upon your undeserving bullseye.

I wish, not for the first time, that there were some means by which I might detach myself from your stagnating posterior, to run away from home as it were, never to return or to be transplanted holus bolus to the rear of a more fastidious master.

If I were asked to recount the most trying period of our uneasy relationship I would plump for that miserable night when you unsuccessfully tried to launch yourself on a singing career. There I was, perilously suspended over the most abominable toilet bowl it had ever been my bitter experience to encounter, when you launched into the opening bars of "South of the Border". I had never heard you sing before. I had heard you humming tunelessly in the background while others joined in the refrain of a popular song but not until that night of the long sitting did you undertake the singing of a complete song.

I remember how I immediately expostulated through the only medium at my disposal. You totally ignored me as was your wont and went on to massacre a score of well-established ditties before exhausting yourself while you sat. You then mercifully submitted yourself to a deep sleep from which you did not wake until a neighbourhood rooster announced the arrival of the new day with a nerve-shattering sequence of cock-a-doodle-doos. I have searched fruitlessly in the hope that I might find something good to say about you before bringing this epistle to a close. There is, alas! nothing for which you might be commended.

Yours faithfully,

Your Rear Aperture.

THE INDEX FINGER OF THE
RIGHT HAND WRITES

Dear Master,

I'll grant you I am but one of ten but you may take it as a Gospel fact that I speak for all. Although you are left-legged you are right-handed and since it is universally accepted that the index finger of the dominant hand has sovereignty over all other fingers, from the thumb to the ludeen, I will take it upon myself, as a natural right, to address you on behalf of all.

The thumb is undoubtedly the bulkiest and the forefinger plays second fiddle to none in matter of length. The ring finger may be the most romantic and the ludeen or little finger the most lovable but it is I who must always point the way.

It is I who taps you on the head and jogs you my master for the resolvement of the prevailing pucker.

By historical and mythological right I am the finger of knowledge, not as an entity but as an instrument of your intent. I listen in respectful silence while the thumb and forefinger clack together for recognition. This is their right. I watch in understanding while the ring finger lights up with pride as the golden band of love is drawn past its knuckle. This is its entitlement. I comprehend when the little finger is gently gnawed by your teeth as you reminisce or ponder. This is its role. They too accept that it is I who must point the way.

Each to his own place as the saying goes and all for the good of the whole. What could be more natural! Naturam expellas furca tamen usque recorret!

Alas and alack I digress! I wish that this were to be a paean of praise on your behalf but the truth is that I can recall little to offset my poor opinion of you, although there were those early days before you willingly submitted yourself to every conceivable form of debauch.

Those early days! I bet you cannot now recall the name of your first love, nay not your first love; rather should I have said your first sweetheart, that angelic sixteen-year-old Lily Lieloly. Oh for the sweet fragrance of her presence once more! Oh to hear her careless, innocent laughter, to savour her heavenly smile! How lovely, lithe and lissom she was, how pure and incorruptible! Whatever happens I shall never forget Lily Lieloly. Moore captures my feelings in his son, "Bendemeer Stream":

No, the roses soon withered that hung o'er the wave
But some blossoms were gathered while freshly

> they shone
> And a dew was distilled from the flowers that gave
> All the fragrance of summer when summer was
> gone.
> Thus memory draws from delight e'er it dies
> An essence that breathes of it many a year;
> Thus bright to my soul as 'twas then to my eyes
> Is the bower on the banks of the calm Bendemeer.

Thus too is the memory of Lily Lieloly to me. Alas poor Moore, so often reviled by ungenerous upstarts because sentiment was his strong suit!

Where was I? It was by a stream, wasn't it, of a summer's evening, as the sun was sinking, as the birds were singing that Lily Lieloly and you sat in a glade near the riverside where the deep, mottled waters reflected the overhanging greenery of beech and sycamore. How could one ever dispel the memory of that sweet, sylvan scene!

That sublime occasion, my dear master, was my finest hour. I remember how a lone linnet took advantage of a lull in the evening chorus and used it to serenade his soulmate as she fluttered and flitted from bramble to bramble, from bower to bower. I recall the doubt in the hazel eyes and trembling lips of lovely Lily Lieloly as she looked unwaveringly into your face and asked if you loved her.

You straightaway cupped her sweet face in your hands and pressed your fingers, of which I was the privileged ringleader, against her silken cheeks. You made comparison of her melting eyes to the deepening cinnamon of the darkening stream, of her ash-blonde hair to the silver beams of the strengthening moon and her bountiful lips to the purest rubies of distant, dusky Arabia.

In those days the poetry would surface in you like the chortling, churning waters of a richly-endowed spring.

"Do you love me, Tommy?" she asked secondly and with myself alone, your faithful index finger, you traced gentle patterns on her now moist lips.

"Love you?" you said, as you pressed me and the others once more to her face. "I love you so much," you whispered fiercely, "that there is a hurt in me which will not heal, a hurt so awful that it pits itself against the very beating of my heart."

You kissed her then but you did not have your way with her because the girl was pure as the morning dew, the evening star, the holy of holies!

That was long ago, Tom, before the pillaging years in their unstoppable succession reduced you to the sorry ould roué that you are today. You did not see Lily Lieloly after that. You allowed yourself to be way-laid by the neighbourhood baggage and so filled were you with shame that you could not look into the hazel eyes of Lily Lieloly ever again.

After that you went from worse to worse, starting off as a devotee of golf club teases and ending as an all-round libertine. Ah but then you married, not alto-gether for love, old boy, but for material possessions and the acquisition of a prime piece of shapely flesh. You fared only moderately in marriage and why should you fare better! You only withdraw what you deposit in the marriage stakes and your romantic deposits were few and far between.

You used me, my master, as you used your business acquaintances and those you called friends, solely for your own ends. You used me, who was clearly meant for better things, for such degrading chores as the evisceration of reluctant mucus securely secreted in the recesses of your puce-veined proboscis, directing me in your urgency to remove not only the recalcitrant snot but also the skin beneath, thereby causing sustained nosebleeds in both nostrils.

I might have been combined, under different circumstances, with my fellow fingers to wield an artist's brush and present the world with a masterpiece or to raise aloft the sword of truth and lead an army of knights against the forces of evil.

I might have, with the aid of your four faithful companions, placed a crown upon your head or if you had only opted for the priestly vows we might have, ultimately, imposed pontifical blessings upon vast congregations and sent them forth across the world with messages of peace and goodwill.

In another age, with another master, I might have drawn your Colt 45 with lightning speed and dispatched to Boot Hill every last desperado in the streets of Laredo!

Had you opted for refereeing I might have pointed goalwards imperiously for the last controversial penalty in the final of the World Cup. Instead I was called upon to scratch your already overscratched posterior.

I might have been the natural baton that conducted the Berlin Philharmonic or, if you had but entered politics, raised myself aloft after your election to the presidency, and confidently pointed the way forward to a better future.

I might have lifted myself to sway a dangerous mob and earned for us unprecedented applause as you silenced the fickle multitudes like a Demosthenes or a Marcus Antonius. But no! You preferred to ditheringly bite my nail when an important decision was called for or point the accusing finger safely at some unfortunate pariah already consigned to damnation.

You had me in every material pie when you might have impaled me on the consciences of the neo-Nazi and the perpetrators of apartheid.

You thrust me into your ear lest you hear whenever an anguished scream shattered the silence of the night. As well as demoting me to the lowly role of snot remover you also transformed me into a vomit inducer and sneeze suppressor.

Worst of all was when you deliberately bypassed grotto, shrine and sacred tabernacle as well as ignoring the last resting places of your forbears when you should have been directing me respectfully to your forehead where I might ceremoniously execute the Sign of the Cross in memory of all things good and holy.

Instead you would titter and scoff with your equally drunken companions when some brave soul dared to cross himself out of deference to the Blessed Trinity.

I'll conclude now in the cherished hope that this

epistle will infuse in you a new determination to devise more edifying pursuits for,

Your ever-faithful,

Index Finger.

THE EYES WRITE

Dear Brain,

We can transmit images of every conceivable kind but our great regret is that we cannot look inward. We cannot be one with our parent, the mind's eye, thereby being in a position to observe on your behalf the wonders and beauties of the world. The mind's eye is your very self, of course, and we are but your servants. We cannot see beyond your mental limitations. We only see what you wish us to see.

. This communication is long overdue by the way and we must say at the outset that it is our contention that our true capacity has never been realised, nor even partially realised chiefly because of your aesthetic shortcomings and your obsession with the carnal.

It became apparent to us at a very early stage that you were no Wordsworth and that your thoughts from youth onwards tended to descend rather than ascend.

You directed us to observe the bosoms and posteriors of golf club teases when we might have been gloriously surveying the beauties of nature. You had us savouring the sonsy swaggers of cheap tarts when we might have been beholding the willowy, fragile forms of delicate demoiselles, the serenity shining on their angel faces, their eyes cast shamefacedly downwards because of the obscene fashion in which you directed us to behold them.

We remember once of an April day you sat by the seashore pondering your future. At the time the world was your oyster and the pain after the rift with Lily was receding as the waves were receding before your very eyes which we have the honour to be.

Your normally turbulent mind had become somewhat becalmed by the gentle motions of the sea for it was a day without wind and the sweet, soothing monotone was a balm to your spirit. We had great hopes for you on that day.

The sky was blue without trace of cloud. On the horizon the smoke from a passing freighter stood like a slender plume in the still air. Seabirds crying joyfully drifted aimlessly overhead and then a curvaceous female appeared out of the waves close by. Without as much as a glance in your direction she unbuttoned the strap of her bathing cap and carelessly flicked her freshly-released curls with expertly-manicured hands.

We did not blame you when you rose from the stone where you had been sitting the better to view this luscious Aphrodite. Just then a soberly-dressed girl with a sweet and gentle face entered the scene. The whole situation was a classical example of your attitude to life and proof, if any was ever needed thereafter, that you were ever a slave to the meretricious.

Both girls were known to you, the bathing beauty casually but the soberly-dressed somewhat more since you had spoken to her and indeed danced with her in the days when you were still rebounding after your Lily Lieloly period.

Of the two we, the eyes, knew that the quality lay with the soberly-dressed and if you had given us our heads, as it were, and allowed us time to dwell on her we might have shown that she was a creature of true loveliness and convey to you the joyful tidings that under the brown costume which she wore was a body as lithe, lovely and desirable as any. Alas you became obsessed as always with the obvious, barely glancing at the clad creature but drooling uncontrollably after the other.

The girl in brown boasted short-cropped, light-brown hair. Her eyes were as blue as the ocean serene which no longer occupied a place in your thoughts. Her smile, as she passed, was radiant and chaste. The two go hand in hand, you know.

The other was prettier on the surface with curling blonde hair, green eyes, rich pouting lips and a burgeoning body designed to infatuate easily-overcome libertines like yourself.

The scene was now set for the drawing back of the curtain. Old Nick must surely have been the stage manager. Possessed with that rare inside knowledge of human weakness and your own particular lack of godliness he rung the bell for the commencement of the play which has been presented on so many strands and beaches over so many years.

As she passed by the soberly-clad girl shortened her steps in the hope that a conversation might be forthcoming because for all your apparent weaknesses she obviously perceived in you some hitherto well-hidden qualities which might one day shape you into a worthwhile human being.

In normal circumstances, if the bikinied beauty was not present, you would have quickly engaged her costumed counterpart for she was a girl of rare and sensitive character. Even you, for all your faults, were aware of this.

Unfortunately you permitted her to pass by and concentrated your gaze on the creature who had emerged from the sea. The water droplets still glistened on her shapely shoulders and when she shook her hair free her body rippled and shivered, stressing her buxom shape and golden hue so that you immediately became sensually enraptured and a prisoner once more of your own inherent prurience. When she waved casually in your direction you bounded like a rutting stag through the shallow water until you found yourself by her side.

How Old Nick must have smiled and how the forces of love and beauty despaired of ever making you see the light! We, your eyes, certainly could not but then you never presented us with the slightest opportunity of doing so.

The play, which was proceeding according to plan under the professional direction of Doctor Darkness, was no tragedy. Neither was it to be a comedy. We would suggest that we were about to witness a traditional farce. We were to be proved right. The vigorous, blooming creature by your side was possessed of a hollow metallic laugh which smote upon the sea's gentle cadences like a whiplash. Your crude jokes were finding their target.

There was no rebuff when your sweaty palm rested on her farthest hip. After all she was not without credentials or so it was believed. What poor girl is not when vile rumour runs unchecked from tongue to scurrilous tongue!

As you moved farther away from the other strollers and bathers you cast us about seeking a place where you might lure her and be hidden from the prying eyes of the crowd.

Suddenly the girl stopped dead in her tracks. Her body trembled and shuddered. Her lips parted and her bosom rose and fell as though she had been seized by a sudden spasm.

What you could not have known, because of failing to employ us to the fullest, was that she had spotted in the distance a lusty young man for whom she entertained the most powerful romantic thoughts. Stupidly taking it for granted that she had succumbed inevitably to your manliness you thrust a hand deep down inside her wispy briefs. The play was coming to its climax. With a well-controlled shriek of disgust she administered a ringing slap to your face, pranced away from you with unconcealed dismay before farting affrightedly in the key of B flat and trotting off through the spray in the direction of the young man who had entered unexpectedly from the wings.

This commonplace farce was not yet ended however. All the pieces were not in place. You stood there in a state of shock for some time until the heady excitement to which you had earlier succumbed was replaced by a feeling of loss and remorse. The sheen which had earlier disported itself on the surface of the sea seemed to have lost its glitter. The seabirds now sang mournfully as though they were keening an irreplaceable loss. The ship had disappeared from the distant horizon and gathering there from the southwest were ramparts of murky clouds which would soon suffuse the shining heavens. You returned to the empty rock from which you had so ardently erupted a short while before, there to ponder life's cruelty before the stormy showers of April would send you scurrying like all the others for shelter.

The farce was about to play itself out in true fashion. All was set for the side-splitting finale which would bespeak the final curtain.

As you sat with your head in your hands, the tears forming in the wells of your eyes, the seabirds dived all about you and it seemed as though they were crying the name of Sheila.

"Sheila, Sheila!" they bleated as they circled immediately over your bent head. Hopefully you raised that same head and listened intently.

"Sheila, Sheila!" they mewed romantically and indeed that was, you imagined, the name of the costumed creature of the short-cropped hair and sensitive face who had passed by and was forsaken by you for the girl who had sallied out of the sea.

"Sheila, Sheila, Sheila!" the white birds called. How's that Gerald Griffin described the seagull:

White bird of the tempest oh beautiful thing!

With the bosom of snow and the motionless wing.

How often have we eyes marvelled at their elegant symmetry and now after delighting you with their fluent and silent flight they would remind you that all was not lost, that there were other fish in the sea. You should have looked before you leaped, however. That is precisely what we humble organs of visions are for, to measure the intervening paces between ourselves and the target and report what lies at the other end so that trouble may be avoided. Utilised thus we are of priceless assistance to our proprietor and will truthfully inform him of every hazard before age eventually curtails us.

In our prime there are no organs to match us. You did not apply us properly when you arose from your stone seat and stumbled crazily off in the direction taken by the costumed Sheila. At first she was nowhere to be seen. You were at a stage then after the stinging rebuff from the bikinied lovely where any form of consolation would suffice. Any port in a storm goes the old adage and thus it was with you as you now lumbered westwards into the sun calling out her name. When you came upon her she was in the arms of another, the first known sympathetic face she encountered after you had spurned her. He was a good-looking chap, lithe and blonde with a confident smile. They both laughed upon beholding your demented

eyes and upon hearing the name Sheila repeatedly is-
suing from your dry lips. Her name it transpired was
Mary Jane. Instantly you retraced your steps angered
and shamed. The seagulls now ululated like banshees
and then mewed derisively as they soared upward and
outward. The rising breeze laughed at your plight and
the freshly whipped breakers roared their appreciation of the farce which had just drawn to its close. It
had been a great afternoon's theatre and how could it
be otherwise with an actor of your stature playing the
role he was born to play and the script ready made for
your unique talents. All nature seemed in uproar,
seas, winds, clouds and rain rendering encore after
encore.

You slunk from what cheerless place a chastened
wretch, a martyr to your baser instincts. We, the eyes,
rallied to your aid, focusing our distracted elements
on the outlines of distant mountains overhung by rich
clusters of white cloud. We left the storm behind us
and the next vista of interest to which we were exposed was the bar of the resort's only hotel.

On your behalf we surveyed the amber contents of
whiskey bottles, the crystal clarity of gins and vodkas,
the shining saffrons, the brighter tambourines and the
pale gold of assorted sherries. The well-stocked
shelves of better-class taverns and hotels are a source
of constant delight to us. The colours of the rainbow
reside in the array of cordials and intoxicants.

The shining bottles, freshly dusted, gleamed and tan-
talised as we took stock of every saleable beverage
from the light chamois of tequila to the green savanna

of crème de menthe. We, eyes, exult in presenting you with this challenging and luminous diversity of exciting colour. Nowhere else will one experience such an uplifting array. We would never object to spending long periods in such prismatic surroundings. We dallied for a period on the cardinal red of Campari and lingered yet again on the mustard of advocaat, flitted to the Russian red of raspberry and finally fixed ourselves on the old reliable amber of honest to God whiskey. The bubbles chortled in the optic as the measure filled. You always drank your whiskey neat but would chase the shorts faithfully with half pints of your favourite ale.

Is it any wonder that soon we were seeing sights that we had not seen before! Eventually we started to see double and the fat, unsmiling barmaid who had dispensed your first drink was now magically transformed into two of the most titillating and identical nymphs ever to stand behind the counter of a tavern. You ignored the printed caution behind the counter which stated:

"When our barmaids start to look beautiful it's time to go home."

Then, of course, you were always a man who never went home when he should. As the barmaid was transformed once more into a single person her beauty decreased not a whit. You told her you loved her and could not live without her but it was a tale she had heard and digested calmly many a time and oft. When you proposed to her she laughed heartily and informed you that she was married already. Shortly after a second proposal and several further declarations of love our vision grew exceedingly blurred. Your hands trembled when you raised your glass. Consequently when you tumbled off the stool and fell in a heap on the floor it came as no surprise to any of the organs involved. The inevitable had happened.

Mercifully, as far as we were concerned, the orgy was ended. We were closed up for the night and would take no further part in the proceedings, nor would we see your mother arrive to collect your drunken remains, but we would open up for business as soon as you had slept it off and we would focus to the best of our impaired ability to see you through the morrow.

This interlude which we have recalled for you is to remind you that we are capable of infinitely loftier undertakings and that you have changed little in the years which have elapsed since that day by the seaside. Nevertheless, we will always be on the look-out for you but would be most appreciative if you could see your way to directing us towards scenes of natural beauty and rapture which abound for man's delight in the world which surrounds you. A time will come when we will be obliged to pull down the shutters forever! It would be a shame if we were not utilised more beneficially before that sad day arrives.

Sincerely,

Your Eyes.

THE GUARDIAN ANGEL WRITES

Dear Brain,

I am the echo of your breath. In quietude, before and after sleep, you may hear me if you are attentive. I should be a consolation, a guarantee that your application for admittance to heaven is still being considered.

I can be terrifying, however, especially when the conscience is justifiably restive after you have perpetrated an evil deed. Then I pulsate and become thunderous in your ears until the guilt drives you from your bed and you pine for instant forgiveness from the evil with which you have become besotted.

Your physical exertions may temporarily silence me but I am always there, always.

Drive me out and you are doomed. You cannot see me because I am not flesh and blood nor am I of the world. At my most visible I am a tiny haze that ups and downs in front of your eyes, that sometimes hangs suspended and moves only in unison with your eyes. Sometimes when you are spiritually pure and possessed of the grace of God, otherwise known as peace of mind, you will catch a glimpse of me in your eyes if you stand before a mirror. Settle for the glimpse for I am not at liberty to reveal myself in full.

I am what you would like to be but cannot because of your human shackles. You are in perpetual bondage to your appetites. I am there to leaven the natural evil which you have inherited. I am the anti-dote for despair. 'Ware these sins above all or I may be driven out; despair, pride and greed and scandalise not the little ones. Remember my friend that you are at this time of life but a russetting leaf. Your summer greenery is long blemished. You could drift down-wards at any time. You would not survive a mortal storm and yet you still persist in bringing the winds of tumult upon your head. You flutter before the endear-ments of mild winds. Imagine your chances in a gale and yet you will persist in gambling with your destiny at this autumnal stage of your lifely proceedings. You would still sport and play beyond the confines of pro-priety as if there was no God. How often have you foolishly told yourself that things will be all right on the day, that the good you have done outweighs the evil. You foolish fellow. It is not you who will be hold-ing the scales.

You are drifting towards the rocks and your barque is a fragile one, already partially decomposed from the buffeting to which you have exposed it over the years. I do what I can and will do what I can but you must improve if I am to be successful in my advocacy. I once heard you say in your devilishly logical way to another drunken companion:

"Why should we be isolated to outer darkness because our so-called saviour suffered for a few hours on a cross?"

He suffered all his life for you and your likes, you insignificant ingrate. Without His arrival the world would be in a state of darkness so terrible that it would be impossible to distinguish it from hell. There would be nothing sacred, nothing to which a man might cling. It is His spirit which maintains the light which is the repository of love, truth, beauty and compassion. Without His perpetual presence you would be less than a shadow.

How often have you denied God as a justification for your self-indulgence.

"There's no God," comes the pitiable bleat from you and other apostles of despair and depravity. Remember that day by the sea when the white breakers foamed and thundered under a blue sky and a rising wind. Your breath was taken away as you gazed enraptured. I stood with you and rejoiced in the glory of God. Remember the old priest who knew you as a boy. He wandered past with his cane and dog.

"Isn't it lovely, Father!" you called out.

"It is indeed, Tommy," he replied gravely. "There is a God there after all."

"What has God got to do with it?" You put the question silently to yourself but that old priest seemed to hear.

"Man didn't make this day," said he. "Nor did he make this scene, and if it wasn't man it can't have been the Board of Works so it has to be somebody else, Tommy."

When your face assumed a slightly mutinous look he spoke again.

"We don't have to call Him God, Tommy. What's in a name, lad?"

He passed by, a smile on his face. Later that day you were to argue in a hotel bar that God was too grave, that there was no humour in the Gospels, that they were the only books from which you never received a laugh. Point taken Tommy. Point taken. The Gospels are full of laughter, Tommy, because they are full of love and truth and these are the fathers and mothers of internal laughter, not the coarse, drunken guffaws which can be heard in public houses and lavatories. Have this laughter by all means but do not deny the existence of the other laughter.

Why do you think nuns go around smiling all the time? Why do so many priests and nuns and other people of God radiate so much laughter? It is because they rejoice in the glory and goodness of the Creator. You know me all your life, Tommy, and yet you do not know me at all because you have never taken the trouble to know me. That is why I now write to you, to beseech you not to dawdle in the mire of debauch while you might be uplifted by goodness and beauty. It is essential that we get to know each other soon so that we might resolve our differences so that I might contribute to the making of the good man you can still be and ought to be. Then would I salute you. Then would I say to the world:

"Come look at my ward, at what he has made of himself, of what he is prepared to be. Come and behold the man who has come in from the darkness and now stands in the light."

I do not expect you to stay in the light, Tom, old son. Just stay as near as you can. I accept your humanity for what it is, a continuing blight for which there is no permanent cure. All I want from you is an honest effort every so often and you will see that the sum of these efforts will pave the way for something outstanding between us, will bring us together as we were never together. It is my bounden duty to ensure that you are set on the road to true enlightenment. If I could accomplish this it would make me a very happy Guardian Angel. It would also make you into something special.

I wonder if you have ever noted certain priests and nuns and other sacred people who quietly yet elegantly shine their ways through a world which is darker than it is bright. Sometime it would be greatly to your benefit if you were to engage briefly in conversation with such people. You would see at once that they are God's people. God lets it be known that they are His people because He shines through them and He has given to their countenances a grace-filled radiance and a loveliness which can be inspiring.

You may if you wish catch glimpses of the Creator in the way these sanctified persons disport themselves, in the way they live and, indeed, in the way they die.

Look to them then and at them and absorb the tranquillity which they generate and you may come to know the true value of yourself. You will not be able to conceive of wrong while you are in their presence. They are to be found everywhere but mostly where there is need for them. They are the unselfish, the concerned, the compassionate, the forgiving. Those are the persons whose presences I always long to encounter.

I know, dear Tommy, that you may never be one of these but by talking to them and perhaps walking with them the meaning of earthly loveliness will be revealed to you. God visits every face but many faces are incapable of hosting Him for any length of time. Others are so steeped in evil that they turn from Him. I saw you turn, Tom, but your ensuing guilt gave me hope for you.

I wish I could precisely define my make-up for you. Firstly I am an angel, probably the most inferior form of angel but an angel nevertheless. I am approved by heaven and I am composed of love and compassion. Also in me is the goodness of the people who went before you, your father, your grandparents, your uncles and aunts and relatives who have gone into heaven, your friends and well-wishers who have followed. All of these are in my make-up and they have empowered me to look after you. In me there can be no evil although I may brush with evil on a daily basis. In me is total well-being for you from the angels and saints of the heavens and the almighty God who watches over all. My commission is to request you to be generous and caring towards your fellow-humans, to be considerate in your treatment of all people from the lowly to the highest and to let love of your fellow man and your God pervade your makeup to such a degree that evil cannot thrive there. Most important of all, of course, is that you should respect yourself.

I am different from the sixth sense in that I have a link with your Creator. The sixth sense is your physical custodian but I am your spiritual custodian. It is my function to preserve you and to present you whole and clean at the end of your days in order to justify my visitation with you and to ensure that you will have as good a chance of salvation as the next man. Nobody knows better than I the terrible burden you have to bear and the temptations that beset you from morning till night. However, you are spiritually well equipped to bear this burden and to resist temptation.

I am your alter ego except that I do not suffer from physical or moral contamination. Pollute me too much by your thoughts or deeds and you will render me ineffective. I am the sacred cocoon through which you would foolishly burst and vanish irretrievably were I not on guard for your sake and yours alone throughout my stay with you.

I will never desert you. If there is desertion you are the one who will do it. By my angelic nature I cannot and will not forsake you. Without me you have no armour against evil. You may escape your conscience from time to time. You may even escape permanently but you will never shrug me off. I will be there at the last day to stand up for you. I ask little in return, just one thing. Few people know, and you are not one of the few, that my feast day occurs on the second day of

137

October. I would ask you to take yourself aside on that day and consider me. Do not pray for me. Rather pray to me. I have no need of prayer being an angel but it is my duty to foster prayer in you. May I say also that I would not be averse to having a few celebratory drinks with you on my feast day provided that you not over-indulge. Still I must concede that I would rather see you half-drunk on my behalf than to suffer the disappointment of your not remembering me at all.

You have never, once in your life, lifted a glass to me. I can accept this from people who do not indulge in intoxicating liquor but it is indefensible that men who drink for every known reason and often for no reason at all are not prepared to toast their Guardian Angel.

Remember my feast day then with prayers for yourself and your own and the salvation of those near and dear to you as well as the salvation of all well-meaning humans on the face of the globe. I am there all right; make no mistake about that. If you have a heart you must admit to a soul and if you have a soul you must admit to a conscience and if you have a conscience you must admit to having a Guardian Angel. All the spiritual aspects and all the physical aspects of the body resemble, in some ways, a deck of playing cards. Some have more value than others but it is the way the cards are played that shows their real importance in the game of life, which is the most bewildering and often most macabre game of all.

There was a night when you stopped to admire a particularly dazzling sky of stars. It was a frosty midnight in the month of December. You had just departed the lovely Lily Lieloly and your young heart was singing. Hearts have been known to sing when love is present and yours is no exception. You marvelled at the magnificence of the midnight sky. That was as close as you ever got to me, Tommy Scam. I was pleased with you that night. I gave you a spiritual pat on the head and endeavoured to infuse in you a greater love of God's creations. The moment passed all too quickly. The gentle images of the stars were driven from your mind by sinister and obscene thoughts of the heavenly creature to whom you had so recently bade goodbye.

I don't know what's to become of you at all. Should you be taken suddenly by a fatal seizure you would be poorly prepared for a confrontation with your maker and even I as a sympathetic go-between would be hard put to defend you. That is why I urgently entreat you to consider your position. Let us look at yesterday alone. There were no morning prayers before you undertook the business of the day. You failed to contribute a full day's work in return for the money you earned. You left your employers short but oh! what an outcry there would be if they left you short!

All through the day you entertained immoral thoughts about the new secretary who occupies a seat directly in front of you; difficult to blame you altogether for this. A young, short skirt and an old and dirty mind are important ingredients in the recipe for sexual debauch of the mental variety. You inflicted continuing harm on your much-abused stomach by

substituting three whiskies for the soup and sand-
wiches which your body so desperately needed and
once you get the taste of whiskey there is no holding
you until total drunkenness sets in. What a way to end
a day! Drunk and insensible, unable to eat the delight-
ful meal which your wife prepared for you and nary a
prayer from your sinful mouth before that intrepid
and often fatal journey though the watches of the
night.

You have always taken more out of the world than
you can every possibly put back into it. Still, as Paul
says: "I will be with you all the days even unto the con-
summation of the world," but after that we may well
find ourselves in a parlous puddle from which there
may be no redemption.

There is still hope, however, as long as I am with
you. You may still aspire and the lower a man has de-
scended the easier it is for him to climb.

I am there to be emulated. Always remember that.
With me as with God all things are possible and the
best thing about God, because of the greatness of His
love, is that He frequently allows Himself to be taken
in by the last-minute repentances of lifelong repro-
bates as long as the sorrow is genuine and the firm resolve to sin no more is present.

Sincerely,

Your Guardian Angel.

THE SIXTH SENSE WRITES

Dear Brain,

Nobody understands more than I the feelings of hopeless frustration festering in the minds of the unemployed millions who stalk the streets of our cities in search of gainful employment. There they are, willing and able to lend their considerable talents and skills to the advancement of the world and its peoples but must languish and despair forever in the awful knowledge that they will never make a meaningful contribution to life nor will they ever develop their natural potential to the full. Thus it is with me.

You, the brain, are my government and like the governments who have knuckled under to unemployment you have denied me my rightful say in your progression. If you had heeded me you might have won the hand of your first love, Lily. There are fateful moments in every man's life when only the sixth sense can direct him, and none more so than when he finds himself in the minefield of premarital miscalculation.

There you were, estimating your chances of an illicit relationship with that lovely and gentle girl when all the time the most inner of intimations were silently suggesting that you would be wise to be at your wariest.

I cautioned you that girls like Lily Lieloly do not come down in every shower, that she was pure of heart and angelic in temperament, that she was sweet and undefileable, but you persisted with your dastardly and foolhardy plot to seduce her.

I recall the setting well and I warned you with every fibre of my make-up that you were treading on dangerous ground. The sixth sense, alas, does not have a physical input to the body. Therefore, I could not seize you by the scruff of the neck as I would have liked and directed you from the wood's shady path to the bright glade.

The bright glade lay by a still stream traversed by hovering kingfishers and flitting water ouzels. Other birds sang sweetly in the surrounding blackthorn and insubstantial summer breezes set the leaves faintly fluttering as the dancing sun ascended the cloud-free heavens. What a setting for a gentle romantic dalliance, a place set aside for handholding and gentle kissing, for promises of lifelong love, promises true but no more, no more.

The shady wood path on the other hand took one away from the shining river and the greensward and lost itself in the shadows and there we stood, the three of us, your lustful self, your laughing-eyed Lily and your sixth sense, crestfallen, rejected and distracted.

You were, without knowing it dear Tom, at the very crossroads of your life and the path you would take on that glorious summer's day would decree the lifestyle that lay ahead of you.

All my components from insight to inspiration were unable to dissuade you from taking the wrong course. In one hand you carried a quart flagon of cider; in the other you lightly held Lily's graceful fingers. For a moment you stood silently, your gaze attracted alternately by light and shade. Lily, for her part, stood dreamy-eyed by your side, not caring which pathway you chose such was her faith in you.

From the very first moment she knew you she had placed her trust in you and now, with the aid of shadow, mossbank and cider you would endeavour to seduce her.

Earlier, in the town, she had protested when you had invested in O'Shonnessy's cider. She had insisted that you purchase a non-alcoholic beverage such as lemonade or orangeade but how airily you had dispelled the innocent girl's doubts as you held up the flagon of amber liquid to the light. Its bubbling, crystal clarity would advertise its harmlessness, protest its innocence and you, you sex-inspired knave, assured her that a body could drink a barrel of it without forfeiting a fragment of control.

O'Shonnessy's Sparkling Cider, and if one was to believe the label it was pressed out of mature and luscious fruit from the home orchard. The home orchard indeed! The world and his wife would swear that nothing but wild crab apples, windfallen and rotten, gathered for pittances by impecunious urchins were its chief if not its sole ingredients.

"My own mother drinks it," you had lied outrageously, knowing that only once ever had she partaken of a small glass after hearing from a now disgraced quack that it had a mollifying effect on arthritis.

Upon hearing of your mother's partiality Lily's remaining doubts were dispelled and she tripped happily by your side till you found yourselves faced with a choice between glade and shade. Winsomely she danced by your side when you led her from the path of brightness.

You knew where you were going for already you had reconnoitred the river banks and their surrounds in search of a suitable spot for what you had in mind. I stayed with you all the time, alerting you and jolting you, vainly trying to remind you that another type of girl would have been far more suitable for the venture in which you would have Lily Lieloly participate. Indeed there are girls in a world of many girls who would require no stimulant such as cider or no secure surrounds for it is part of their nature to indulge such as you.

Lily was different as were most of the girls of your youth. You knew this and yet you gambled a lifetime in her presence for a lustful interlude.

You stopped at a dark pool over which hung the long green arm of a leafy chestnut. Alongside there grew a man-sized cushion of spring, spongy, white-green moss. Without more ado you uncorked the

cider and held the jowel to the untainted lips of Lily
Lieloly. Poor child she spluttered and choked but
sport that she was she swallowed nevertheless. You
drank copiously yourself and then you implanted a
gentle kiss on the upturned face of your first love. You
made her drink again and again as you did yourself
until the bottle fell from your hand and rolled without
a tinkle into the long grasses close by. Then you knelt
and you drew Lily downwards also, cupping her heavenly face in your common hands as you drew her slender body close to your own and eventually side by side
on the mossy bed. No birds sang in that loveless place
and no breeze dared enter its clammy confines. The
pool darkened as your body hardened and your desire
took hold. Was there ever anything as lovely as Lily's
blushing face before she realised for what evil business
you had lured her into the shadows. You should have
desisted from your purpose when that first faint
flicker of alarm puckered her lovely brow and you
should have begged her forgiveness when the initial
shock became transformed into sheer terror. You
should have released her, asked for her forgiveness
and lain your lapse at the door of your unbridled manhood. She would have forgiven you. She was that kind
of girl. But no, you forced your inflamed kisses on lips
that now curled inward in disgust. You ripped her
blouse apart and her beautiful breasts of the dun-dark
nipples shivered and trembled from the unaccus-
tomed exposure. She covered them with her shaking
hands at which point you grasped her scantily-clad
buttocks in your insensitive palms. She cried out

asking you to restrain yourself but her pleas fell on deaf ears. How fortunate she was that you always had extreme difficulty in unbuttoning and unzipping the flaps of those cheap trousers of yours. She made good her escape as you tried frantically to rip the offending zip apart but it remained stuck. Knowing she had gone, your passion subsided as quickly as it had erupted. When the heinousness of what you had tried to do dawned on you you threw yourself on the mossy bed, face downwards, in a fit of remorse.

You might have had Lily Lieloly and her splendid, burgeoning breasts and her warm lips on yours and the silken subtlety of her white, pulsing body and all the incomparable intoxicating gifts which only a sweet, loving woman can bestow upon a man. You might have known heaven on earth if you had only heeded your sixth sense. I was and am one of the most price-less acquisitions a body can have. I must be heeded, however, if I am to remain sharp.

After that inglorious encounter with the girl you lost forever, I wilted somewhat and was for a long while the despair of the other senses who, capable as they are, cannot maintain the harmony of the human system without my presence. I am convinced that the sunless clearing where you contrived to trap her was not an evil place before you selected it for your dark deed. All it had before you polluted it was the poten-tial for evil. I can tell because I have the means of pin-pointing locations where evil may surface. After your departure from that place you left much of your innate wickedness behind you, that innate inheritance

146

which is the scourge of every human. There it became absorbed into the bloomy surroundings, transforming them into a setting so accursed and malevolent that other sixth senses would be immediately alerted to its dangers thereafter. Places such as that unfortunate clearing are not evil in themselves. Only man has the capacity to generate evil into them and, in so doing, partially purifies himself.

After Lily you degenerated further, rallied briefly to a state of moderate goodness and later became for all time the very epitome of fallibility. You began to need me desperately after a while and you had the maturity to heed me.

There was the time of the bull. You walked through a morning field searching for mushrooms with your eldest daughter. Her happiness was reflected in you, in you who deserved nothing of that ilk, but she loved you. Then the good God in His mercy and generosity acknowledged that love and permitted the beauty of her young soul to temporarily shine on yours. As you both dallied now and then to pluck a mushroom from its loamy bed the dew flickered on the green grass and the cobwebs beaded with tiny drops glittered like diamond broaches in the sunlight.

It was a happy time and then, suddenly, as you straightened to add a mushroom to your store you sensed, through me, that danger had materialised behind you. Without me you would have been quite incapable of registering any such recognition. You stiffened but did not look round. This was the correct thing to do under the circumstances. Your other instincts wanted you to bolt, in fact insisted you quit the scene without wasting a thought on your defenceless daughter. Human love, however, which makes a mockery of terror and danger when it flowers to its fullest, spoke on your behalf:

"Run," you whispered urgently. "Run to the gate. Climb it and don't look behind. Off with you now."

Dutiful daughter that she was she did as you bade. She would, without question, have walked over a clifftop had you commanded her. Behind you came the terrifying sound of scraws being uprooted. You knew then that you were being seriously considered for dispatch to eternity by Drumgooley's bull, a ferocious creature whose presence in the vicinity you should have taken into account before your risked you and your daughter's lives to satisfy your craving for mushrooms.

With soiled trousers and dyed hairs standing rigidly atop your head you tiptoed gatewards at what you hoped was a leisurely pace. Then came the bestial, ear-splitting bellow which precipitated the charge. The race was on! The gate, only fifty yards away, seemed like miles. You were obliged to hold your paunch in your hands as you ran lest its downward plopping bring you to the ground and certain death. Your pursuer was in his prime. His rippling back spoke of his splendid condition but the bloodshot eyes were crazed and the brain tormented from the sapping services he had rendered to two score hederaceous cows and heifers from early summer. You panted as you ran. He snorted as he neared his victim. With the gate still yards away you stumbled but did not fall. Alas the distance between you and the bull was considerably shortened by this reverse. Only inches now divided you. Then you heard your daughter's voice:

"Come on, Daddy!" she screamed, and with a super-human effort you managed to clamber over the gate, breaking your wrist as a result.

The bull, a lusty three-year-old of the Aberdeen Angus strain, pawed the ground inside the gate and lofted clay and sods over his powerful shoulders. Never did a daughter cling to a father with such fervent love. Never did so many warm tears rain on such a bristly face. Even you, perverted apology for a man that you are, were moved. Even I whose sole business is to issue warnings and cautions was prepared to concede at that moment that maybe you were not a full one hundred percent bad.

You met another crossroads when taking the wrong turning could have cost you your life. As always I was vigilant. You stood outside the shoddy entrance to Madame Sin Su's Palace of Peking Pleasures in one of the seamier side streets of Soho. Madame Sin Su, Mistress of Euphemism. Who else but a Mancunian streetwalker could think up such a name! A short while before you had availed yourself of the services available behind the tottering facade that fronted the palace and now you stood undecided, not knowing whether to go left or right. The right seemed to be safer. The street was well-lit. There was a policeman standing at the end some distance away. This was the route for which you opted until I took a hand and imposed my restraining influences with all my might upon you. You heeded me and proceeded to the left. You may truly thank your sixth sense for having survived that night. The policeman was not what he seemed. Rather was he part of a gang of professional muggers who would cheerfully slit your throat for a sixpence. Knowing your penchant for preserving your finances you would most certainly have resisted or run off if that were possible. Either way would have been fatal.

There was the time you had the ink-wetted pen in your hand ready to sign on the dotted line of a contract which you believed would guarantee you vast profits. In a thrice, at my bidding and without explanation to anybody, you had laid the pen down and refused to sign. Subsequently you learned that you would have lost all if you had added your signature. In spite of all I have done for you I doubt if you are even aware of my existence. I might not be visible or tangible but I am worth my weight in gold as any fairminded man would admit. Please acknowledge.

Sincerely,

Your Sixth Sense.

THE CONSCIENCE WRITES
TO THE BRAIN

Dear Brain,

How about a little of your undivided attention? Up until this time, as far as I am concerned, your undivided attention has been scarcest of all identifiable commodities. You may well ask again as you have so often asked in the past in your own coarse fashion:

"Who the hell are you?"

I'll tell you who I am. I am that little inner voice which endeavours to tell you how to distinguish between right and wrong so that your whole being might come belatedly to know peace and tranquillity.

I am also the spirit of unrest and I will dog you to the end of your days. You have never been certain about my exact whereabouts and I have often heard you ask: "Where the hell are you?" I am everywhere that you are but chiefly I reside in you although I have been known to make pilgrimages to your heart.

Often you have asked in frustration: "What the hell are you?"

A religious person might call me the law of God written in the heart of every human. A layman might call me the judge and jury of human behaviour insofar as it relates to one person.

I know that I have caused you some anguish although not nearly enough because your spiritual hide is almost impervious to my proddings and prickings. I do unsettle you somewhat, however.

It's not that I wish to unhinge you altogether. That is not my function. Only you have the power to unhinge yourself and alas! how often has the disorganised brain ended life prematurely with bullet, poison, rope or water according to prevailing tastes or contiguity of one or other of this gruesome four! Conscience hath not made cowards of these poor demented creatures. Rather have we invested them with the lunatic courage to commit the unthinkable lest they commit the ultimate upon those they love and cause the greater folly.

Now to you! I have found you to be morally unconscious mostly in your self-induced sexual deliriums although aided and abetted by responsive partners.

I have found you to be frequently deaf in your responses to my queries regarding your financial dealings but I have found you at your most declamatory when others do unto you as you would unto them.

I have lived with you since you attained to the use of reason which, in your case, was somewhat delayed beyond the normal maturing stage. As you developed into manhood you gradually tried to refine me to a state where I would be subject to your will and failing this made subtler bids in an effort to get me to work in the same harness as your will. Will and conscience can never be bedfellows, so your bid failed.

It was these failures which brought you to that inevitable state at which all humans arrive sooner or later when they cannot dominate me. Then comes the painful realisation that I must somehow be salved and placated.

An agreement between you and I became a necessity but in that pact you would continually try to deceive me, although your need for total forgiveness was always paramount in your thinking. Without it you were ever on edge, sleepless, restive, incapable of self-consolation and self-forgiveness.

Self-forgiveness. There's a tricky one. Must man be shriven by outside agents or is the capacity to absolve himself within himself and is this legitimate in the sight of God? I am only the conscience and cannot say but it would make my work less complicated if there was an answer forthcoming.

I would be in favour of self-forgiveness where the brain, prompted by the heart, has already forgiven others. A man who has forgiven all those who have wronged him, however little or however mightily, should have the power to forgive himself.

It is not a power I would confer on all men, only on those whose natures are so forgiving that they would not even dream of withholding forgiveness from those who would ruin and destroy them.

The great question that arises here is my future in the event of your being consigned to damnation or hell or whatever. Being your conscience I am part of you, the most in-built part of you, the greatest single influence for good within the entire framework of your make-up. Am I, who has performed Trojan heroics in my efforts to guide you aright, to be dispatched to hell with you or am I to be segregated from the rest of the personality and sent aloft? Am I alone to be delivered, as it were, while my heart and my spirit and yourself and my all, are consigned to everlasting and excruciating obscurity?

What becomes of consciences like me when you no longer function? Must I, who am not to blame, reside in hell with you or am I to be disposed to a limbo? If so you will be only partially in hell and I will be only partially in this new limbo or will I be received into heaven high and dry on my lonesome?

This in my estimation would constitute a forced breaking-up of the spiritual fundamentals, which I would hold to be illegitimate, and I must hereby advise you that it is your bounden duty to instruct your vocal cords so that they might express my views clearly and loudly to the responsible authorities and, thereby, avoid the reckless sundering of our very self.

Failing that, you might have your right hand address itself to notepaper where my views would be clearly set forth without embellishment; copies then to be made and dispatched to the more responsible newspapers in the hope that a sharp controversy might ensue which would eventually lead to badly-needed clarification on this vexatious topic.

To return to your innate immorality for which, on account of your human make-up, I do not hold you fully responsible although I always have and still do expect better from you. If only you could relate me equitably to your body's and mind's demands, there would be little need for recrimination on my part. I hate the use of the word salve but I daresay I would be somewhat salved.

Remember too that an act which might painfully prick one conscience often has no effect whatsoever on another, so that you cannot expect to be guided by the complacency of another, so-called just man, after that person has perpetrated an evil act. The complacency does not reduce the abhorrence that should exist in you, dear brain.

There are consciences and consciences. There's the Christian conscience, the Catholic conscience, the Mohammedan conscience; the Atheistic, often the most tormenting of all; there is the Pagan conscience, the Greek Orthodox conscience and the Buddhist, and the whole shooting gallery of sects, factions and assorted conventicles, all making different and often lunatic demands upon their respective proprietors. However, in the final reckoning it is the individual conscience that matters.

You may be impressed or intimidated by local conscience, by national conscience and by international conscience but while these are fine in themselves and while they reform for the better and highlight ills and evils you are still left with me. There are also some comic aspects of conscience which may not seem in the least comic to their adherents.

In the western hemisphere a man may possess only one woman at a time while under the public eye but in the East he may possess as many as he likes. There is no way of reconciling these two consciences although the over-riding feature of both may be the search for simple truth as it is known to both, the everlasting aspiration towards goodness and eventually a cherished berth in the heaven of the hereafter.

I am forever promoting the fear of hell and hope of heaven since, because of teaching and tradition, you, the brain, cannot conceive of anything else in the uncharted territories beyond the grave. Therefore, I speak to you of things which are already established solidly within yourself, things such as heaven, hell and purgatory. Each human brain, without exception, is possessed of all three and endures all three in his passage to his destiny so maybe that's the end of it or is it that these three are extended into the hereafter? I prefer to suggest that occasional hell, frequent purgatory and too little heaven are the dominant features of a comprehensive human life, so that the hereafter, if any, should provide a predominance of heaven for every Tom, Dick and Harry who has passed this hazardous way, who upon entry to this often God-forsaken world is immediately impregnated with insurmountable prejudice, greed, intolerance, bigotry and all the other countless faults so rampant and ever-fermenting in you, the human brain.

As your conscience it is my duty to point out these things as it is your duty to acknowledge and weigh them against your more edifying activities. I ask you to ponder on all that I have conveyed to you, all for your future good I might add. Finally, I must inform you of one inescapable truth against which there can be no real argument, so take heed!

You may repent and recant privately and publicly until you are blue in the face. You may be publicly and privately forgiven of all that you have publicly and privately confessed but remember that it is with me you will have to contend at the end of the day, and if I don't give you the nod all your penitential posturings will count for naught.

As ever,

Your Conscience.

John B. Keane **The Bodhrán Makers**

"This powerful and poignant novel provides John B. Keane with a passport to the highest levels of Irish literature ... an important and invaluable book which must be read by all who love Ireland." The *Irish Press*

"A tale that goes straight to the heart – the heart of the reader as well as the heart of the matter. Keane gets beneath the skin of Irish culture, past and present, and provides a view tourists will never see." *Bloomsbury Review*

"Told with a vigour and vivacity which keep the attention riveted." *The Irish Times*

"A thorough, pained, loving account of a lost world – with the novel itself an act of cultural survival." *Kirkus Review*

Paperback £4.95

John B. Keane **Power of the Word**

"John B. Keane, poet, playwright and philosopher, is a national treasure and has been gambolling amongst words to good effect for years. Here he is on the joys of country life, free-range love and public affairs, to name but a few." *Ireland of the Welcomes*

Paperback £3.95

John B. Keane: **Owl Sandwiches**

"Wherever you read in this slim volume you find wit and vivacity, and darn good entertainment by a master craftsman." *Derry Journal*
"It is the kind of book which would tempt you to read snippets aloud when the hilarity becomes too great to bear alone." *Ireland's Own*
"This book is Keane at his best." *Cork Examiner*
"As always John B. Keane is good fun, his eye may be sharp for the more idiotic foibles of humankind but he writes with warmth and kindliness... He describes Ireland in a manner guaranteed to pour balm into the nostalgic heart of the exile." *Irish Democrat*

Paperback £5.95

John B. Keane **Man of the Triple Name**

"Hugely enjoyable." *In Dublin*
"Anybody who enjoys old-style storytelling at its best should reach for *Man of the Triple Name*." *Irish Post*
"This lyrical, most human and highly humorous book." *The Irish Times*

Paperback £4.95